Christian and Humanist Foundations for Statistical Inference

Christian and Humanist Foundations for Statistical Inference

Religious Control of Statistical Paradigms

ANDREW M. HARTLEY

RESOURCE *Publications* · Eugene, Oregon

CHRISTIAN AND HUMANIST FOUNDATIONS FOR
STATISTICAL INFERENCE
Religious Control of Statistical Paradigms

Copyright © 2008 Andrew M. Hartley. All rights reserved.
Except for brief quotations in critical publications or reviews,
no part of this book may be reproduced in any manner without
prior written permission from the publisher. Write: Permissions,
Wipf and Stock, 199 W. 8th Ave., Suite 3, Eugene, OR 97401.

ISBN 13: 978-1-55635-549-3

Manufactured in the U.S.A.

All scripture quotations, unless otherwise indicated, are
taken from the HOLY BIBLE, NEW INTERNATIONAL
VERSION®. NIV®. Copyright © 1973, 1978, 1984 by
International Bible Society. Used by permission of Zondervan.
All rights reserved.

Contents

Preface / vii
Acknowledgments / xi

1. Motivation and Direction of This Book / 1
2. Statistical Inference and Scientific Induction / 13
3. Paradigms for Statistical Inference / 18
4. The Philosophy of the Law Idea (PLI)—A Summary / 54
5. The Nature Ideal, Mathematicism, and Statistical Inference / 68
6. The Personality Ideal, Subjectivism, and Statistical Inference / 74
7. The PLI and Subjective Bayesianism / 81
8. A Paradigmatic Synthesis / 96
9. Conclusions / 107

Glossary / 113
Bibliography / 119

Preface

A HOST of books, lectures, journal articles, and even college courses have discussed various types of associations between religion and science. They have dealt with

- whether religious beliefs and findings of science support or undermine each other;
- the use of scientific conclusions to illustrate spiritual truths;
- differences in the types of questions religion and science can answer—teleological and normative questions versus predictive and descriptive ones, for instance;
- ethical implications and responsible uses of scientific conclusions;
- influences of the moral values of scientists on theory making;

and a broad range of other topics.

The Philosophy of the Law Idea (PLI), developed by certain Christian theologians and philosophers, focuses on a different type of relation between religion and science. It shows how religious beliefs are beliefs about the self-existent and self-sufficient. It goes on to analyze the ways these beliefs regulate all scientific theorizing, arguing that this regulation is "the most basic feature of the science-religion relation."[1] The Christian Bible declares that "the fear of the Lord is

---

1. Clouser, "Replies," 27.

the beginning of wisdom,"[2] and that knowing God enriched the Corinthian Christians in "all (their) knowledge."[3] On the basis of these and many other Bible verses addressing wisdom and knowledge, the PLI holds that having the right God is a necessary foundation for every scientific endeavor. It studies how religious beliefs influence scientific theories. Moreover, it shows that, if theories are not controlled by Christian beliefs, they are controlled by non-Christian ones.

Yet, the PLI does not advise scientists to rely on religious beliefs and books to answer whatever questions they might have, as if, for instance, the Bible could serve as a science textbook. Rather, as I will explain, religious beliefs control science in an indirect manner—they set bounds for overviews of reality which, similarly, set bounds for scientific theorizing. Such overviews, also called ontologies, try to discover and disclose the essential nature of reality. They are concerned with what kinds of things exist and with the connections between the various types of properties and laws in human experience.

If all scientific and, in particular, all statistical theorizing is controlled by religious beliefs through overviews of reality, and if, as Abraham Kuyper emphasized, "There is not a square inch in the whole domain of our human existence over which Christ, who is Sovereign over all, does not cry: 'Mine!'"[4] then obedience to Christ requires at least two responses from those of us who plan, generate, or use statistical inferences. First, we need to identify the overviews which are implied by or, at minimum, consistent with, Christian belief. Second, we must seek to align our statistical inferences with those overviews. I aim, therefore,

2. Prov 1:7.
3. 1 Cor 1:5.
4. Kuyper College, "About Kuyper."

in this essay, to examine ways religious beliefs control statistical theorizing.

With this book I intend to speak to a wide audience. Hence, the book presupposes no prior knowledge of statistical concepts or procedures; however, familiarity with the most commonly used concepts and procedures would certainly facilitate the reading. In particular, some knowledge of the main theoretic systems of statistics, frequentism and bayesianism, would be useful. A short glossary of statistical and other terms appears at the end the book.

I believe that readers specializing in various sciences will find this essay helpful. Primary among them are Christian statistical analysts, meaning Christians who design, perform, and report the findings of inferential statistical analyses. We might call them "statisticians;" however, any use of that label must not be taken to imply that all statistical analysts hold college degrees or occupational titles in statistics. More generally, all statistical analysts, and not only Christian ones, would profit from thinking about the implications of religious beliefs for statistics.

A second group of potential readers is the community of philosophers of statistics. I propose that tracing philosophical theories about the purposes and nature of statistical inference back to their religious roots, as I will attempt here, contributes to explaining why these theories diverge from one another. Indeed, the PLI claims that, in philosophical debates in general, "one receives the impression that [proponents of different schools of thought] are reasoning at cross purposes, because they are not able to find a way to penetrate to each other's true starting-points. The latter are masked by the dogma concerning the autonomy of theoretic thought." This is why "a Thomist has never succeeded by purely theoretical arguments in convincing a Kantian or a positivist of the tenability of a theoretical metaphysics. Conversely, the Kantian epistemology has not succeeded in winning over a single believing Thomist to critical idealism."[5] This "dogma concerning the autonomy of theoretical thought" is, I suggest, responsible as well for the difficulties bayesians and frequentists usually experience in trying to convert each other to their own points of view.

Those who may not plan or conduct statistical analyses, but nonetheless interpret and use the statistical inferences which others have published, could also benefit from this discourse. Admittedly, unless they are funding statistical analyses, they often have little control over the design and conduct of those analyses. They can, however, investigate and understand the religious foundations of statistical arguments, equipping themselves to more accurately judge those arguments in light of their own religious beliefs and overviews of reality.

Others who may find this essay useful are thinkers in other academic or professional fields who wish to examine the religious foundations of those fields. A chemist, for instance, may be interested in the relations between religious beliefs and his or her theorizing. It is my hope that he or she might glean some ideas from this essay, as well as works of Basden, Clouser, Dooyeweerd, Strauss (see Bibliography), and others, concerning religious beliefs which have provided the underpinnings for various schools of thought within chemistry.

---

5. Dooyeweerd, *New Critique*, I, 35.

Acknowledgments

I AM grateful to the many who contributed directly or indirectly to this essay; without their efforts, it never could have been completed. Special thanks to

John R Britton who, although too humble to admit it now, introduced to me and embodied for me Christ the Savior and Lord, in his conversation as well as his personal affairs.

The staff of the Coalition for Christian Outreach, Pittsburgh, Pennsylvania, who, during my undergraduate years, taught me the importance of submitting every area of my life, including my academic discipline, to Christ.

Drs. Roy Clouser and Bruce Wearne who, in their books and journal articles, in meetings with me, and in countless pages of correspondence, explained to me many features of the Philosophy of the Law Idea (PLI), evaluated my impressions and prose concerning what the PLI might indicate about statistics, suggested areas for improvement, and encouraged me at every step of constructing this essay.

Dr. Steven Preston, who introduced me to the philosophy of statistics and the bayesian-frequentist controversies.

Paul Robinson, who made numerous helpful comments on the manuscript.

Dr. Russ Wolfinger who, time after time, bolstered my confidence to proceed with this work, forwarded me important resources, recommended new areas of research and, when the need arose, plied me for clearer lines of reasoning.

My parents who, directly and indirectly, taught me to read, to write and, most significantly, to love.

1

Motivation and Direction of This Book

THE CHRISTIAN Bible declares that variation is everywhere in creation, and it all comes from the Lord God:

> How many are your works, O Lord!
> In wisdom you made them all;
> The earth is full of your creatures.
> There is the sea, vast and spacious,
> Teeming with creatures beyond number—
> Living things both large and small.[1]

Thanks to this great diversity, the branches of science will probably never run out of creatures to "number." It seems plausible that there will always be new things to discover in our creaturely tasks of ruling over the works of God's hands[2] and "subduing" all the earth,[3] "working and taking care" of the garden,[4] and naming all the living things.[5] John Calvin recorded that the variation within creation is certainly sufficient to keep us busy for a lifetime:

1. Ps 104:24–25.
2. Ps 8:6–8.
3. Gen 1:26, 28.
4. Gen 2:15.
5. Gen 2:19–20.

> To the same purpose is the narration of Moses, that the work of God was completed, not in one moment, but in six days. For by this circumstance also we are called away from all false deities to the only true God, who distributed his work into six days, that it might not be tedious to us to occupy the whole of life in the consideration . . . [W]hithersoever we turn our eyes, they are constrained to behold the works of God . . .[6]

Yet, too, one can hardly deny that all that variation makes these "caretaking" responsibilities less straightforward. For, variation leads unavoidably to uncertainty and complexity in the way we classify, associate, and make predictions from day to day. Torrance, summarizing the work of Polanyi, says, "[A]s we explore the universe in our scientific activities, it keeps on surprising us, disclosing to us patterns and structures of an indefinite range of intelligibility, which we could never anticipate on our own . . . The universe constantly takes us by surprise in this way because it is correlated to the infinite, inexhaustible freedom and rationality of the Creator."[7] Many states of the world and many consequences from whatever actions humans might plan cannot be specified with complete certainty. In such situations, the special sciences often call upon the discipline of statistics to take uncertainty into account in some ordered way. Statistics serves these sciences by investigating hypotheses about the world and the likely results of potential actions. We might say it is the science which deals specifically with uncertainty in quantitative contexts. Insofar as workers in those other sciences truly concern themselves with their "caretaking" responsibilities, statisticians seek to work with them to achieve the greatest good possible. There

---

6. Calvin, *Institutes*, I, xiv, 2.
7. Torrance, *Ground and Grammar*, 59.

is much evidence, then, that God ordained statistics as an area of investigation, and that He calls men and women into it for His purposes.

Does the Christian faith have anything distinctive to say, though, about the foundations or practice of statistics as a science? To suggest that being a Christian should influence how one works in any science may surprise some scholars. Many hold that religion is neutral with respect to science, in the sense that one's religion does not, or need not, affect one's scientific activities. These convictions were popularized by Descartes and Bacon, two prominent fathers of modern rationalism and empiricism, respectively:

> Briefly, the tradition of the objective [religious and philosophical] neutrality of scientific activity is based on two initially separate streams of thought. There was the earlier Cartesian tradition in which man, by applying pure reason alone and by divesting himself of all ideas of which he was doubtful, could arrive at a few central ideas concerning which there was absolutely no doubt. . . . The second tradition stemmed from Francis Bacon and others, and is usually designated as British Empiricism. In this view, experimentation and observation of nature was the primary condition for arriving at objective truth . . . Both these traditions are obviously based on man's autonomy in creation, in a faith in man's ability to obtain true knowledge in one of these ways, or what in fact turns out to be a synthesis of these traditions. However, even when the emptiness of either of these ways of achieving true knowledge was pointed out by Hume in England and later Kant in Germany, and a new method of philosophy was introduced which saw more clearly the interplay of man's reason and experience, this

synthesis was still based on man's autonomy, the independence of man's reasoning and scientific activity from any religious or philosophical preconceptions.[8]

In short, Western Civilization has a long tradition of thinking of the sciences—especially the so-called "abstract" or "formal" sciences such as mathematics, logic, and statistics—as religiously neutral.

These judgments notwithstanding, some have indeed identified connections between Christian faith and the sciences, including even the natural sciences. Chase and Jongsma list a large number of papers and books on links between Christianity and the mathematical sciences, for example.[9]

In fact, the religious control of all theorizing within some other scientific fields has already received much literary attention. Addressing the science of applied mathematics, for example, Strauss disclosed the religious nature of philosophical presuppositions about number and quantity, and showed how these presuppositions lead to differing conclusions as to the level of exactness that can be found in mathematics, the possibility of mathematical "facts," the existence and meaning of the infinite, the relationship of mathematics to logic, and other topics central to the philosophy and applications of mathematics.[10] He also revealed effects of religious beliefs on theorizing within physics and biology. Dooyeweerd, on the other hand, reflected seriously on the foundations of various "social sciences"—law, society, economics, and politics—showing that religiously-motivated assumptions in these sciences lead to conflicting theories within them.[11] Moreover, Basden not only discussed

8. Brouwer, "Commitment and Theories," 1–2.//
9. Chase and Jongsma, "Bibliography."
10. Strauss, *Paradigms*.
11. Skillen, "Dooyeweerd's Contribution," 20.

the religious roots of theories in information systems (IS), but also argued persuasively that theories in IS consistent with the PLI's overview of reality would vastly improve the returns the world is to realize from investments in IS.[12]

Does the religious control of scientific theorizing carry over, however, to the specific science of statistical inference? Statisticians, biologists, physicists, chemists, educators, economists, and other scientists engage in this type of inference to make and corroborate statements about averages, trends, proportions, risks, variation, and so forth, based on observed quantitative data. The vast majority of these scientists who have as much as thought about the relations between religion and science regard statistical inference as religiously neutral.

People's reasons vary for believing statistical theorizing is independent from religious beliefs. Many thinkers expect statistical inference to lead automatically to truth, regardless of religious presuppositions, on account of statistics' heavy use of mathematics. In their view, a firm grounding in quantitative reasoning affords statistics complete reliability, evenhandedness, and objectivity. These scientists therefore regard statistical inference as an unbiased judge of evidence, an impartial instrument for determining facts.

Other scientists who consider statistics to be religiously neutral think the individual researcher is, or should be, at liberty to arrive at his or her own conclusions regarding statistical hypotheses. They set the researcher at liberty to mentally mingle statistical calculations together with other, non-statistical information, according to preferences, general impressions, and "states of mind." They allow the researcher the freedom to decide by how much the data support or contradict the hypotheses of interest. This intuitive process

---

12. Basden, *Christian Philosophy*.

is expected to lead the researcher to private and personal, yet valid and comprehensible, experiences of statistical data.

In what follows, I will not only challenge these arguments that statistical inference is religiously neutral; I will argue that these dogmas even expose underlying religious beliefs. First, the argument that statistical inference is completely objective due to its mathematical foundations evinces a belief in the complete trustworthiness of quantitative reasoning, over and against other types of human experience; that belief, I will show, is ultimately religious. Second, underlying the willingness to regard the individual researcher as the final judge of scientific truth is a presupposition that scientific truths are less interpersonal and objective, and more personal and subjective. This presupposition rests on a religious belief that has located the source of the orderliness of human experience in the mind of the knowing subject, rather than, say, in the laws by which God sustains the universe.

Looking carefully at the religious roots of theories in statistical inference is vital, because scientific researchers in a wide variety of fields, including economics, biology, physics, and more, rely heavily on this kind of inference: "Whenever noisy data is a major concern, scientists depend on statistical inference to pursue nature's mysteries."[13] They routinely cite p-values, confidence intervals, hypothesis test results (see Glossary for these and other technical terms) and other statistical outcomes as evidence, and sometimes even conclusive proofs, for their theories. Hubbard and Armstrong even singled out the statistical significance test, in particular, as the "glue that binds together the entire research process," in that this test

> largely dictates how we formulate hypotheses; design questionnaires; organize experiments; and analyze, report, and summarize results. It is

---

13. Efron, "Modern science," Abstract.

viewed not only as our chief vehicle for making *statistical* inferences, but for drawing *scientific* inferences, too . . . This test, in short, is no mere statistical 'technique,' but instead is seen to lie at the heart of the way in which we conceptualize and conduct research.[14]

What is more, R. A. Fisher's *Statistical Methods for Research Workers*, arguably the most influential statistics book ever published, asserted that statistics is the principal means by which certain other fields "may be raised to the rank of sciences."[15]

In light of how often scientists depend on statistical inference to substantiate their claims, it is more than a little disconcerting that veteran as well as neophyte scientists routinely misinterpret ordinary statistical results. Even more worrisome is the fact that, though these results are offered as so-called "evaluations" or "assessments" of scientific hypotheses, they actually address quite different matters. In this essay, I discuss the most popular statistical outcomes, along with some of their putative meanings and implications. I then explore why, over the last century, statisticians have continued to implement these outcomes. In particular, I argue, based on an analysis of how religious beliefs control scientific theorizing, that many of the misinterpretations of statistical results arise because, in large part, statistics has been controlled by non-Christian, humanist religious beliefs. That analysis is provided by the PLI.

Where, though, does one begin such an investigation? One obvious area in which to expect this control to manifest itself is in debates, both between statisticians and between philosophers of statistics, regarding why and how to perform statistical inference. For that reason, in much of

14. Hubbard and Armstrong, "Why we don't know," 115.
15. Fisher, *Statistical Methods for Research Workers,* First Edition, 2.

this essay I will examine two divergent and wide-ranging streams of thought concerning the proper ways to go about statistical inference: bayesianism and frequentism. I will deal also with some of the seemingly intractable controversies between those who advocate one or another of these sets of principles, and look at some controversies within these statistical camps.

Bayesianism and frequentism each can be regarded as a moderately homogeneous collection of theories about what can be concluded about scientific theories, given empirical data. They can too, however, be divided further into four relatively cohesive paradigms, or systems of theories, of statistical inference: objective and subjective bayesianism, and what I identify as direct and indirect frequentism. I will explain what each of these paradigms prescribes concerning the planning, performance, and interpretation of statistical analyses. The controversies between them have given rise to literally hundreds of written works from the 1920s until the present. These works record in some detail the standpoints of the paradigms concerning the types of concerns statistical inference can address, the information it can use and the calculations it can implement. As a statistician in the United States pharmaceutical industry, and an observer of the statistical methodologies applied in other industries and fields of research, I have witnessed some of the pivotal practical implications of these standpoints. I will explain how these implications evince many effects of religious beliefs on statistical inferences, in even the simplest applications of statistics.

Consider, for instance, one of the most straightforward experiments imaginable, an experiment conducted to study the credibility of the hypothesis (let us call it H) that, on any single future flip of a particular coin, the coin will come to rest in the heads-up position. The experiment consists of two stages. In Stage 1, a mechanical engineer inspects the physical characteristics of the coin, and finds no reason to suppose the coin is not fair; that is, the engineer does not judge the coin to be biased in any particular direction. In Stage 2, the coin is flipped 20 times and 12 heads are obtained.

In the course of my arguments, it will become apparent that bayesian and frequentist statistical perspectives, themselves under the control of religious beliefs, affect a variety of features of the inferences potentially following such an experiment, including

- The types of questions about H one can expect statistical inference to answer.

- The admissibility, or lack of it, of the physical evidence about the coin (in other words, the coin's apparent fairness).

- If the physical evidence is deemed admissible, the manner in which it may be combined with the quantitative data, that is, with the 12 heads obtained from the 20 flips. In particular, should that evidence be combined with those data according to the judgment and intuition of the researcher, or according to mathematical laws?

- The weight that is assigned to the physical evidence collected in Stage 1, vis-à-vis the weight assigned to the quantitative data collected in Stage 2.

- The relevance, if any, of the manner in which the experimenters came to flip the coin 20 times, not more and not less. Say, for example, that the experimenters decided to stop flipping as soon as they had obtained 12 heads, rather than stopping when they had performed 20 flips. Religious beliefs impact whether the researchers must account, in statistical inference, for this so-called "stopping rule."

- The permissibility of different scientists coming to different conclusions about H.
- The post-experimental level of trustworthiness or credibility of H.

With respect to all these features and more, statistical inference is anything but religiously neutral.

This essay proceeds as follows. Chapter 2 introduces statistical inference as a science, paying particular attention to the kind of questions statistical inference seeks to answer. Chapter 3 describes the four popular paradigms, or systems of theories, mentioned above regarding what may be inferred with reference to scientific hypotheses, based on data. Direct frequentism and objective bayesianism produce certainties, or degrees of belief, of hypotheses using only empirical observations and mathematical reasoning; they disqualify as non-scientific such other considerations as pre-experimental opinions and expert knowledge. Indirect frequentism calls on the researcher to freely and informally order the data and other forms of evidence into an intelligible overall experience. Subjective bayesianism depends on empirical data to modify pre-experimental (or, more generally, pre-analytic) certainties of hypotheses according to mathematical laws.

In Chapter 4, I introduce some premises and conclusions of the PLI. First, I focus on that philosophy's account of how religious beliefs regulate scientific theorizing, which is "the most deeply pervasive feature of the religion-science relation, and the key to understanding the Biblical claim about all truth depending on having the right God."[16] I then describe two Christian religious beliefs that have implications for overviews of reality: the belief that only God is divine, meaning that nothing but God is self-existent and self-sufficient; and the belief that all of creation depends di-

---

16. Clouser, "General relation."

rectly on Him. I next explore the overview of reality the PLI promotes, which fits into the philosophical bounds set by those Christian beliefs. This overview considers the various kinds of properties and laws in human experience to be mutually irreducible and yet interconnected. It shows that, as a consequence of these relations between the kinds of properties and laws, the type of experience it calls "prescientific" is the indispensable foundation for scientific knowledge.

Chapter 4 also describes the PLI's analysis of two humanist religious belief systems: the ideals of "nature" and "personality." Although each of these ideals is humanist, in the sense of treating specific features of humanness as divine, the ideals nonetheless oppose each other. The nature ideal regards humans' quantitative and logical facilities as sufficient for processing empirical data and ascertaining natural laws and properties. The personality ideal, in contrast, sees the world as an arena for freely revealing and exploring the human personality, an arena in which individuals need be obedient to themselves only.

In Chapters 5 and 6 of this essay, I review two other overviews of reality studied by the PLI, which could be called varieties of "mathematicism" and "subjectivism," respectively. The former is consistent with the humanist nature ideal, and the latter with the humanist personality ideal. I show that subjective bayesianism matches the bounds for scientific theories set by the PLI's overview of reality, in two primary respects: Its calculations employ empirical data to enhance, rather than replace, prescientific experience; and it respects the coherence posited by the PLI between quantitative properties and laws and so-called fiduciary properties and laws. Indirect frequentism, on the other hand, fits the bounds set by the aforementioned subjectivism. Finally, the two other paradigms, objective bayesianism and direct frequentism, fit the bounds set by mathematicism.

Chapter 7 identifies some other features of subjective bayesianism that allow it to harmonize well with the PLI's overview of reality. In Chapter 8, I outline conditions under which the standard tools of frequentism and objective bayesianism may be implemented, despite the inconsistencies between the PLI's overview of reality and those paradigms.

Lastly, Chapter 9 summarizes the essay, noting some common patterns among statistical paradigms that fail to match the PLI's overview. This chapter also suggests some directions for further work in tracing the ways religious beliefs influence statistical inference.

2

Statistical Inference and Scientific Induction

THE AMERICAN Statistical Association (ASA) offers two definitions of statistics as a discipline:
- The science of learning from data (from Jon Ketternring, ASA President, 1997)
- The mathematics of the collection, organization, and interpretation of numerical data, especially the analysis of population characteristics by inference from sampling (from the Merriam-Webster's Collegiate Dictionary)[1]

The ASA also portrays statisticians working on such tasks as "determining what information is reliable and which predictions can be trusted." Two branches of statistics that deal with information and predictions in these ways are statistical inference and statistical decision analysis. Statistical decision theory deals with prudent or sensible actions in the presence of uncertainty. It works to calculate the likely quantitative losses and gains associated with various potential courses of action, when those losses and gains cannot be predicted precisely. Usually, once a decision analysis is complete, the decision maker makes the decision that minimizes the expected net loss (or maximizes the expected net gain).

1. American Statistical Association, "What is statistics?"

On the other hand, this essay concentrates on statistical inference. This inference is usually portrayed as a method of making statements as to the truth, falsehood, plausibility, credibility, likelihood, or probability of statistical hypotheses, given observed quantitative data.[2] Here, a statistical hypothesis is, in general, a proposition, phrased in logical terms, that is true or false but is not known to be true or false. It could specify, for example, that a particular medical patient is afflicted by a particular disease, or that one medical treatment is more effective than another, or that a war will break out next year between a certain country and another.

Statistical hypotheses are often stated in more formal terms as propositions about statistical parameters. A statistical parameter is, in short, an unknown quantity of interest that influences the probability distribution of the data (the statistics) planned to be observed. Thus, the data can inform the researcher about the parameter, but do not unequivocally identify it. The average amount of time each child of a particular country in a specified age range watches television each week, the proportion of airline flights that will depart later than scheduled next year, the most probable increase in crop yield resulting from the use of a certain novel fertilizer, and the number of hurricanes in Florida of a certain minimum intensity this coming August can all be statistical parameters. So, for instance, two statistical hypotheses phrased as propositions about statistical parameters might state that "the average number of nails manufactured daily at this factory is 3 million," or "at one atmosphere of pressure, the boiling temperature of this new chemical solution is less than 60°C."

Usually, the statements statistical inference makes about hypotheses are phrased in terms of levels of certainties

2. Fisher, *Statistical Methods for Research Workers,* First Edition, 1; Berger, *Statistical Decision Theory*, 7; Kocher and Zurakowski, "Clinical epidemiology and biostatistics."

Statistical Inference and Scientific Induction　15

and beliefs. Say that we wish to investigate the aforementioned hypothesis *H* that the boiling temperature is less than 60°C. In an experiment to assist with such an investigation, we might gradually heat 100 test tubes full of the new solution, in 100 separate ovens, and record the temperature at which each test-tube-full of solution boils. We could then use statistical methods to analyze the recorded temperatures, possibly together with other information, in such a way as to establish some justifiable degree of certainty, probability, likelihood, or degree of belief in *H*.

Statistical inference is usually conceived, then, as an attempt to answer questions of the following general form:

Given observed quantitative data, how credible is a scientific hypothesis of interest?

This "central question of statistical inference," as I will call it, is relevant in a wide variety of circumstances; the ASA mentions collecting information from a sample and extending the results to an entire population, for instance. As another example,[3] to which we will refer repeatedly in the following chapters, consider a scientist who wants to assess whether a particular object has Attribute *A* (hypothesis H_1) or not (hypothesis H_0). She submits the object to an experiment for detecting *A*. The experiment returns a positive result (which I will denote by $+T$) for *A*. She knows that, in this situation, $Pr(+T|H_1)$, the probability of $+T$ given H_1, is 0.80, and $Pr(-T|H_0)$, the probability of a negative result ($-T$) given H_0, is 0.95. Neither of these probabilities is 1.00, so that whatever the experimental result, neither H_0 nor H_1 is established unequivocally. The best she can aim for is some degree of certainty or belief about these hypotheses.

There is, admittedly, an "error-frequency" school of thought within the discipline of statistics, which attempts to test hypotheses in order to manage so-called "inductive

3. Hartley, "Philosophy of law idea and role."

behavior." Some among this school might disagree with the particular phrasing of the "central question" above. Chapter 3 will attend to "inductive behavior" in more detail. In the present context, however, it suffices to say that the originators of this school emphatically excluded statistical inference from their purview, saying that their "hypothesis testing" method has nothing to do with making statements about hypotheses.[4]

What I have named the central question of statistical inference is, like most scientific questions, inductive; it asks what can be concluded about a hypothesis (a proposition about an unknown state of affairs), based on known observations. The inductive character of statistical inference is evident throughout the statistical literature. Huntsberger, for example, defines statistical inference as "generalizing from the part to the whole. Given incomplete information (from the sample), [it] is making a statement about the larger group from which the sample was taken."[5] According to *The Orthopaedic Journal at Harvard Medical School*, the purpose of statistical hypothesis testing is "to permit generalizations from a sample to the population from which it came."[6] *A fortiori*, Anderson says more inclusively that "statistics [itself] is one means of inferring generalities from specific observations, and it is objective."[7] The distinction between induction and deduction, another form of argumentation, will prove important to keep in mind, in later discussions of differences between bayesian and frequentist paradigms.

The above experiment concerning Attribute *A* exemplifies statistical testing, the most commonly applied statistical procedure for evaluating hypotheses in light of data.

4. Neyman and Pearson, "On the problem."
5. Huntsberger, *Elements of Statistical*, 5
6. Kocher and Zurakowski, "Clinical epidemiology and biostatistics."
7. Anderson, *Practical Statistics,* 3.

Despite the popularity of this testing, however, the levels of certainty of hypotheses (such as H_0 and H_1) that test results (such as $+T$) are supposed to justify, generate, or support are the center of a protracted controversy between various statistical paradigms, which I review next.

3
Paradigms for Statistical Inference

SCIENTISTS ACCUSTOMED to substantiating their claims using statistical results are often surprised to learn that several conflicting paradigms for statistical inference are now in use. Any such paradigm is a system of theories concerning what may be concluded about statistical hypotheses, given statistical data. It prescribes a set of answers to the central question of statistical inference I have specified above. Here, I describe some key elements of four statistical paradigms, each of which has captured the following of large numbers of statisticians and other scientists.

Direct Frequentism

Two popular paradigms for statistical inference are called "frequentist," because they express their results in terms of how frequently this or that type of data would be observed, in hypothetical repetitions of the data gathering procedure, assuming this or that hypothesis is true.[1] Let us refer to the experiment in Chapter 2, for instance, in which a scientist investigates whether an object has Attribute A. There, the datum is $+T$, and a frequentist might report the result

$$Pr(+T|H_0) = 1 - Pr(-T|H_0) = 1 - 0.95 = 0.05,$$

1. Diamond and Kaul, "Prior Convictions."

which indicates, in repeated testing, how often $+T$ would be observed assuming H_0.

One such frequency of data is the p-value p, the outcome of so-called "significance testing" and the most ubiquitous statistical result reported in nearly every field where statistics is applied.[2] It is calculated as follows[3]: First, the researcher selects some hypothesis H to be tested and determines what data, if observed, would to some degree undermine or contradict H. The researcher then calculates the probability distribution $f(x|H)$ of the data x, over hypothetical repetitions of the experiment and assuming H is true. Subsequently, the data are collected and, using $f(x|H)$, the researcher determines p as the relative frequency of data at least as contradictory to H as are x, in those repetitions. In short, p expresses the probability, assuming H, of data "as extreme" as x, in imaginary replications of the experiment that was performed. As I will explain, interpretations of p vary widely; however, in general, the smaller is p, the more the researcher tends to "reject" H or, at least, consider H untrustworthy.

Mathematically speaking, frequencies of data such as p are not inferences, because they are statements about data, not about hypotheses. Nonetheless, the two frequentist paradigms I will describe do offer them as inferences. The first, which can be called "direct frequentism," takes these frequencies to indicate directly conclusions about hypotheses. Once a test is designed, this paradigm insists that conclusions hinge only on these frequencies. A conclusion, in this sense, could state whether a tested hypothesis

---

2. Addressing medical research, for instance, Salsburg ("Religion of Statistics," 220) writes, "After 17 years of interacting with physicians, I have come to realize that [to] many of them, . . . [s]tatistics refers to the seeking out and interpretation of p-values." Similarly, Gigerenzer ("Superego, ego," 315) charged that "significance testing . . . eventually became the backbone of institutionalized statistics in psychology."

3. Berger and Berry, "Statistical Analysis," 164.

is likely or trustworthy. It could also state a degree to which the hypothesis is likely or trustworthy. In either case, direct frequentism portrays statistics as an objective, "automatic technology."[4] It therefore stands in striking contrast to another form of frequentism I will describe in the next section, an "indirect" frequentism which brings together frequencies of data with extra-experimental considerations such as experts' judgments or the outcomes of previous studies.

Some writers explain direct frequentism by likening it to the deductive syllogism known as "*modus tollens*" or "disproof by contradiction" within classical logic.[5] Logically, if an event E cannot occur if hypothesis H is true, and yet E is observed, then H is refuted or, as Popper famously said, "falsified."[6] Formally, this form of argument appears as:

1. Major Premise: H implies $-E$.
2. Minor Premise: E.
3. Conclusion: $-H$.

In this example, $-E$ and $-H$ are read as "not-E" and "not-H," respectively.

Statistical hypotheses cannot be evaluated using *modus tollens*, because they are non-deterministic; they do not predict uniquely the data that will or will not occur, but rather the probability of each type of data. Nonetheless, direct frequentist conventions prescribe the falsifying or "rejection" of these hypotheses in a manner similar to *modus tollens*. For that reason, this paradigm is often said to constitute a type of hypothetico-deductive, falsificationist

---

4. Schuurman, "Beyond empirical turn;" Sterne, "Teaching hypothesis tests," 991.

5. Batanero, "Controversies;" Berger and Berry, "Statistical analysis," 161.

6. Popper, *Logic of Scientific*.

reasoning.[7] Here's how direct frequentism works to reject some statistical hypothesis H:

1. Major Premise: Datum E, if H is true, is "sufficiently improbable;" in other words, $Pr(E|H)$ is "sufficiently small."
2. Minor Premise: An experiment is run, and E is observed.
3. Conclusion: H is rejected, and the statistician is supposed to declare that "statistical significance" has been attained.

If E is observed, then, the statistician is to reckon H not credible or, at least, act as if H were false.[8] By convention, E is usually considered "sufficiently improbable" if $Pr(E|H)$ is 5% or less. In the experiment above for detecting Attribute A, for example, the datum $+T$ was observed. Since $Pr(+T|H_0)=5\%$, $+T$ is sufficiently improbable. The scientist must, then, reject H_0 and declare that the object has A.

Conventions aside, though, once one rejects a hypothesis, what can one justifiably conclude about its credibility? This is to ask, what inferential meanings about hypotheses does a frequentist test result truly convey? Answering this question is not at all straightforward. For, as stated earlier, the probabilities of frequentist tests, like the $Pr(+T|H_1)$ and $Pr(-T|H_0)$ above, are frequencies of data assuming this or that hypothesis, instead of degrees of certainty about hypotheses given observations. They are deductive statements, rather than the inductive statements that would constitute statistical inference. To arrive at inferences, frequentism

7. Ellison, "Statistics and Science," 364.

8. Ware, "P-values," 154; Maksoudian, *Probability and Statistics*, 221–232; Hogg and Tanis, *Probability and Statistics*, 394–99. Fisher ("Statistical methods and scientific induction," 39) justified this inferential process by saying, "Either a rare event has occurred, or H is false." *Obscurum per obscurius*.

must, one way or another, transmute these deductive frequencies into inductive levels of certainty, as alchemy tries to synthesize gold from base metals.

At least two direct frequentist traditions for generating these certainties can be discerned. First is a particular type of interpretation of the results of what Jerzey Neyman and Egon Pearson (N-P) named hypothesis testing. In this interpretation, the scientist calculates the hypothesis test results and, from two pre-specified statistical hypotheses, chooses the hypothesis to be credible or trustworthy.[9] The following portrayal of this testing is typical:

> Any statistical test of hypotheses works in exactly the same way and is composed of the same essential elements:
>
> 1. null hypothesis
> 2. alternative hypothesis
> 3. test statistic
> 4. rejection region
>
> . . . If for a particular sample the computed value of the test statistic falls in the rejection region, we reject the null hypothesis and accept the alternative hypothesis. If the value of the test statistic does not fall into the rejection region, we accept the null hypothesis.[10]

Here, the "test statistic" is some summary of the data, such as a sample mean, median, p-value, or sample variance. This conception of statistical testing is direct frequentist because it depicts the statistical conclusion following directly from the test result.

---

9. Huntsberger, *Elements of Statistical*, 141–47, Anderson, *Practical Statistics*, 52; Maksoudian, *Probability and Statistics*; Kocher and Zurakowski, "Clinical epidemiology and biostatistics."

10. Mendenhall et al., *Mathematical Statistics*, 383.

Paradigms for Statistical Inference 23

Now, N-P developed hypothesis testing in the 1930s "to introduce some hard logic, as opposed to informal judgment, to ideas of significance testing."[11] They prescribed these tests as rules for what they called "inductive behavior" (decision making) only.[12] They explicitly warned against using test results to make inferences about hypotheses, claiming that "[n]o test based upon a theory of probability can by itself provide any valuable evidence of the truth or falsehood of a hypothesis."[13]

Later direct frequentist authors describing N-P's hypothesis testing, though, blur the line between hypothesis testing and inference, in at least three ways. First, they do not mention N-P's admonition against drawing inferences from hypothesis test results. Second, what is worse, they even discuss hypothesis testing under textbook sections entitled "statistical inference" and the like. Ignoring N-P's warnings, they implicitly, at least, attach epistemic meanings to hypothesis test results.

Ryan is typical in this regard; he offers an entire book chapter entitled "Statistical Inference: Estimation and Testing," which presents hypothesis testing among other methods.[14] Predictably, then, the reader (who has probably been taught something about statistical inference being, as Huntsberger said, "generalizing from the part to the whole"[15]) often supposes that a hypothesis, once rejected by a hypothesis test, is unlikely, implausible, improbable, or at least untrustworthy. Guilford, too, in what was "probably the most widely read textbook in the 1940s and 1950s,"[16]

   11. Goodman, "p-value fallacy;" Kempthorne, "Of what use," 764.
   12. Hubbard and Armstrong, "Why we don't know."
   13. Neyman and Pearson, "On the Problem."
   14. Ryan, *A short course*, 3–1.
   15. Huntsberger, *Elements of Statistical,* 5.
   16. Gigerenzer, "Superego, ego," 323.

encouraged students to read epistemic meaning into hypothesis test results: "If the result comes out one way, the hypothesis is probably correct; if it comes out another way, the hypothesis is probably wrong."[17] Even professional statisticians habitually make inferences in response to hypothesis test results; Holzinger, for example, promotes such an interpretation of a goodness-of-fit test when he advises, "Unless the value of [p] be *0.2* or more, the fit cannot be regarded as good and other curves should be tried."[18]

A third manner in which authors attach epistemic meaning to N-P hypothesis test results is by associating them with "statistical evidence." Kinnear and Taylor, for instance, make such an association by portraying statistical test results as evidence in a marketing research text that discusses N-P hypothesis testing at length but does not even mention significance or other forms of statistical testing.[19] As another example, in Chapter 2, I already noted how *The Orthopaedic Journal at Harvard Medical School* identifies the purpose of hypothesis testing as inductive generalization.[20]

However, the commonest frequentist tradition of reading statistical test results, many writers have claimed, is to take one probability or another of the observations as the post-experimental probability of, or at least a level of confidence in, a hypothesis of interest.[21] Some authors have even substantiated such claims with empirical studies.[22] In these

17. Guilford, *Fundamental Statistics,* 156.

18. Holzinger, *Statistical Methods,* 247.

19. Kinnear and Taylor, *Marketing Research.*

20. Kocher and Zurakowski, "Clinical epidemiology and biostatistics."

21. Davidoff, "Standing statistics," 1019; DeGroot, "Doing what comes naturally;" Pratt, "Bayesian interpretation."

22. Oakes, *Statistical Inference,* 82; D'Agostini, "Confidence Limits;" Diamond and Forrester, "Clinical trials and statistical verd.icts," 385; Diamond and Kaul, "Prior Convictions," Banatero,

studies, students, statisticians, and scientists were asked to interpret statistical test results. Large proportions of the respondents and, often, majorities of them, reinterpreted probabilities of data as probabilities rather of hypotheses, even as recently as 2002.[23]

Let us consider four examples of the indirect frequentist custom of construing the probability of observed data given a hypothesis as signifying, or at least indicating something about, the plausibility of a hypothesis given data. First, in the experiment in Chapter 2, this custom might lead to reading the deductive $Pr(+T| H_0)$ as the inductive probability $Pr(H_0|+T)$. If the scientist conducting that experiment reasoned this way, she would conclude that, given the positive test result $+T$, she is 95% certain that the object has Attribute A. Second, the United States Federal Register, 50 CFR Part 17 interprets p as the probability of a hypothesis, when it takes $p=0.20$ as implying "an 80 percent probability of true nonzero trends."[24] As a third instance, most non-statisticians and even many statisticians think p is the post-experimental probability of the tested hypothesis.[25] Among these is Lee who claims that, "[w]ith $X^2=10.17$ and two degrees of freedom [$p<0.01$], the probability that the three absolute infiltrate groups have the same response rate is less than 0.01."[26] All these epistemic interpretations of statistical results seem attributable, at least in part, to Fisher's contention that "[f]rom a test of significance . . . we have a genuine measure of the

---

"Controversies," 82.

23. Haller and Krauss, "Misinterpretations."

24. US Federal Register, "Rules and regulations," 13097.

25. Berger and Berry, "Statistical analysis," 162; Goodman, "p-value fallacy," 997.

26. Lee, *Survival*, 288.

confidence with which any particular opinion may be held, in view of our particular data."[27]

Fourth, many authors believe that p (which, as mentioned above, is a probability about data) indicates whether "the differences [between treatment groups] could be due to chance."[28] This belief has even been institutionalized, to some extent, by certain journal editorial staffs who mandate that authors interpret p as indicating either whether "it is likely the results observed are due to chance"[29] or "the probability that the apparent success was due to chance."[30] Also popularizing this belief has been the *Center for Health Evidence*, which states, "[t]he more significant the test, the less likely it is that the observed differences . . . are due to chance alone."[31] Now, the results of an experiment are due to chance alone if and only if the tested hypothesis is true;[32] therefore, when a researcher implies that p reveals the probability the results are due to chance alone, he also implies that p reveals the probability of the tested hypothesis.

Scientific literature is replete, then, with reinterpretations of frequentist test results (that is, of frequencies of data) as inductive statements about the plausibility of a hypothesis given data. Such appraisals might seem natural enough; however, they are not only mathematically unjustified, but flat wrong. They exemplify the misunderstanding that $Pr(H|x)=Pr(x|H)$ for any hypothesis H and datum x.

27. Fisher, *Statistical Methods for Research Workers*, 1st ed., 74.

28. Journal of Thoracic and Cardiovascular, "Statistical methods," 2A; McDaniel and Gates, *Marketing Research*, 537; Kocher and Zurakowski, "Clinical epidemiology and biostatistics."

29. Kocher and Zurakowski, "Clinical epidemiology and biostatistics."

30. Barnes, "General acceptance," 322.

31. Oxman et al., "How to use an overview."

32. Leaving aside such philosophical matters as whether chance exists, or the nature of chance.

Various thinkers have called this misunderstanding the "transposition of conditioning"[33] or the "fallacy of the transposed conditional."[34] Gigerenzer calls it the "Bayesian id's wishful thinking"[35] since, as will be shown later in this chapter, Bayesian reasoning provides the degrees of belief in hypotheses that scientists desire and suppose they can obtain from frequentist test results.

The transposition of conditioning often carries grave consequences, for $Pr(H|x)$ and $Pr(x|H)$ could differ widely. Kolmogorov's definition of conditional probability, which is almost universally accepted, implies that $Pr(H|x)=Pr(x|H)[Pr(H) / Pr(x)]$. Therefore, the transposition of conditioning, expressed as $Pr(H|x)=Pr(x|H)$, is inaccurate quantitatively to the extent that the bracketed quotient $[Pr(H) / Pr(x)]$ differs from unity.

To illustrate the potential difference between $Pr(H|x)$ and $Pr(x|H)$, consider two probabilities that might arise in a medical diagnostic setting. Suppose a patient presents himself with spots on the skin, and the physician seeks to evaluate whether the patient has measles. The physician might characterize this evaluation as pinpointing the probability $Pr(measles|spots)$ of the hypothesis that "the patient has measles," in light of the observable datum that "the patient has spots on the skin." He must, however, carefully distinguish $Pr(measles|spots)$ from $Pr(spots|measles)$. Plainly, $Pr(spots|measles)$ is close to 100% since almost everyone with measles develops spots; $Pr(measles|spots)$, though, falls far short of 100% since many common medical conditions

---

33. Berger, *Statistical Decision Theory*, 120; Berger and Sellke, "Testing a point null;" Davidoff, "Standing statistics," 1020; Goodman, "p-value fallacy" and "Bayes factor."

34. Batanero, "Controversies," 89.

35. Gigerenzer, "Superego, ego," 330.

besides measles could result in spots. Transposing the conditioning can, then, lead to egregiously inaccurate inferences.

I pointed out above that many authors explain direct frequentist reasoning by reference to logical disproof by contradiction. Similarly, transposing the conditional can be explained by likening it to the logical fallacy known as "affirming the consequent," which has the following syllogistic form:

1. Major Premise: *H* implies *E*.
2. Minor Premise: *E*.
3. Conclusion: *H*.

The conclusion of affirming the consequent is plainly invalid, for *H* could be false even if *E* is true. Yet, that fallacy closely resembles transposing the conditional,[36] which can be expressed as follows:

1. Major Premise: *Pr(E|H)=p*; that is, *H*, if true, implies *E* has probability *p*.
2. Minor Premise: *E*.
3. Conclusion: *Pr(H|E)=p*; that is, *E* implies *H* has probability *p*.

Granted, a well-taught introductory statistics course will warn students against transposing the conditioning of any conditional probability. However, despite the careful instruction of countless statistics instructors, most frequentist results are interpreted using the transposition of conditioning and its variants.

Another example of this transposition is the way direct frequentism interprets so-called "maximum likelihood estimates" (MLEs). Researchers often collect data *x* to estimate a statistical parameter μ ("mu") that is "unknown" in the sense that the parameter's precise value is not determined. They often use the method of maximum likelihood (ML)

36. Ibid, 85.

estimation in such cases to identify the value of μ which maximizes the deductive likelihood *Pr(x|μ)*. This value is called the MLE of μ. Not much seems wrong with MLEs themselves from a purely mathematical perspective;[37] each MLE merely confers the greatest probability on *x*.

The mathematics of ML estimation and MLEs are completely silent, though, about three basic questions: What should one suppose that each MLE signifies about μ, why should one think of the MLE as inferentially relevant and, therefore, why would one maximize the likelihood? On account of such silence, some authors describing MLEs do hint at answers to these questions, by introducing MLEs in textbook sections and chapters entitled "Statistical Inference," and the like. Others connect MLEs with statistical inference more explicitly, including those who call the MLE a "good estimate"[38] of μ. Fisher even stated that "everyone knows" the MLE is the "best estimate"[39] for μ. Most writers on general linear models and linear regression analysis teach the same nowadays, when they promote the MLE as the "best linear unbiased estimator."[40] Collectively, these authors insinuate the MLE is the inductively most credible value of μ, as if it maximized not only *Pr(x|μ)* but—transposing the conditioning—*Pr(μ|x)* as well.[41] This interpretation, like most uses of the transposition of conditioning, is direct frequentist, since it takes the data,

---

37. As will become apparent, however, insofar as calling them ML *estimators* casts them as valid inferences about hypotheses and parameters, such casting is unjustified.

38. For instance, Hogg and Craig, *Introduction to Mathematical*, 202.

39. Efron, "RA Fisher," 97.

40. E.g., Montgomery et al., *Introduction to Linear*, 21.

41. Wright, "Making friends with your data," 124; DeGroot, "Doing what comes naturally."

mathematically manipulated, to directly indicate conclusions about parameters.

Despite such claims about MLEs, these results are not necessarily the best estimates of statistical parameters, and the recklessness of uncritically considering them as such is serious enough to underscore with an example. Imagine that the coin-tossing experiment cited in the preface was conducted to estimate the chance of heads, μ, for a particular coin that, upon physical inspection, is apparently fair. We flip the coin *20* times, and observe *x=12* heads. Now, the MLE of μ is *0.6*, since *0.6* maximizes *Pr(x|μ)*; every other potential value of μ confers on *x=12* a lower probability than does *0.6*. It seems silly, though, to conclude on the basis of this reasoning alone, as does the direct frequentist, that *0.6* constitutes the best estimate for or most credible value of μ; surely, our initial assessment of the coin as apparently fair should count for something. Thus, ML estimation, at least when it is regarded as a form of statistical inference, lacks some crucial element.

Certain interpretations of MLEs, then, perpetrate the transposition of conditioning. This transposition arises even more often, however, when (as already mentioned) a significance test's p-value *p* is read inferentially as the postexperimental probability *Pr(H|x)* of the tested hypothesis *H*.[42] Mathematically, *p* is a probability about data; it is not a (inductive) probability of *H*. Mindful of the potential difference between *Pr(H|x)* and *Pr(x|H)*, as illustrated above with reference to measles and spots, we should not be surprised that *p* can differ markedly from *Pr(H|x)*. As a matter of fact, however small *p* may be, *Pr(H|x)* could exceed even *50%*.[43]

---

42. Goodman, "p-value fallacy," 997; Oakes, *Statistical Inference*; Davidoff, "Standing statistics," 1019; Berger, *Statistical Decision Theory*, 120.

43. Berger and Sellke, "Testing a point null," 111.

Thus, declaring whether *H* is plausible or not solely on the basis of *p* seems rather presumptuous.

Such declarations exemplify, however, what direct frequentism aims to do: derive inductive certainties about hypotheses directly from deductive frequencies of data. I have described how these derivations are attempted in hypothesis testing, ML estimation and significance testing. I will assert, in later chapters, that this tendency stems from certain presuppositions about what constitutes necessary and adequate grounds for scientific conclusions, and that these presuppositions have their roots in humanist religious beliefs.

Indirect Frequentism

Direct frequentism rigidly interprets statistical results as automatic, objective conclusions implied by mathematical and logical rules. Its most popular alternative, what I will call "indirect frequentism," in contrast, allows the scientist to freely and creatively "decide by how much a theoretical proposition has been advanced by the data,"[44] when processed by the "constructive imagination."[45]

Indirect frequentism is propounded by thinkers like Sterne and Smith, who would have us "move from the [direct frequentist] idea that results are significant or non-significant to the interpretation of findings in the context of the type of study and other available evidence."[46] Peto et al. echo this sentiment; without getting specific at all, they counsel researchers to somehow combine "prior opinion and knowledge with p-values to guess the truth."[47] Motulsky, in the same spirit, responds to his own question, "What conclusion

44. Cohen, "Things I have learned."
45. Gigerenzer, "Superego, ego," 320.
46. Sterne and Smith, "Sifting the evidence."
47. Peto et al., "Design and analysis," 595.

[from the p-value] should you reach?" in indirect frequentist fashion, saying merely, "That's up to you. Statistical calculations provide the p-value. You have to interpret it."[48]

Reflecting a similar attitude, McLean denounces the direct frequentist practice of considering claims "to have been established, or not, according to whether they [are] significant at the *5%* level, or at the *1%* level. This misuse of hypothesis testing has led to results with *p=0.049* accepted, and those with *p=0.051* rejected, and is one of the major reasons for the controversy of the last half century."[49] He then pinpoints the essence of what I mean by indirect frequentism: "Statistics is about judgment, and ironclad rules such as these discount the role of judgment."

Moreover, Sterne deems an indirect frequentist stance important enough to state and restate in the same article: "[O]ur students . . . will . . . need to interpret the results of particular analyses in the light of wider knowledge as, for example, when a patient, faced with the latest health care, asks for advice on whether they need to change their treatment or their lifestyle"[50]. . ."For these reasons, our teaching of statistical inference should continue to move away from decisions based on statistical significance and towards interpretation of results based on both the statistical analysis (confidence interval and p-value) and wider considerations."[51]

Indirect frequentism's foremost champion, despite his equivocations between direct frequentism and indirect frequentism over the course of his career,[52] has been R.A. Fisher, who some regard as "the hero of twentieth Century

48. Motulsky, *Intuitive Biostatistics,* 96.
49. McLean, "On the nature and role," 15.
50. Sterne, "Teaching hypothesis tests," 989.
51. Ibid, 991.
52. Gigerenzer, "Superego, ego," 318.

statistics."[53] Fisher placed great importance on "the right of other free minds to utilize [statistical results] in making their own decisions."[54] Perhaps because of that conception of the statistician's autonomy, he promoted using an "intuition for statistical inference,"[55] in light of "what seems not improbable," "common sense," and one's "state of mind"[56] to combine statistical outcomes—especially, the p-value, p—informally with other considerations:

> Fisher proposed [p] as an informal index to be used as a measure of discrepancy between the data and the null hypothesis. It was not part of a formal inferential method. Fisher suggested that it be used as part of the fluid, non-quantifiable process of drawing conclusions from observations, a process that included combining [p] in some unspecified way with background information.[57]

According to more recent writers, expanding on Fisher's work, such "background information" might include

- estimates of magnitudes of effects,[58]
- results of other studies[59] and
- the "prior plausibility of the hypothesis under test and the desired impact of the results."[60]

---

53. McLean, "On the nature and role."
54. Fisher, "Statistical methods and scientific induction," 77.
55. Efron, "RA Fisher," 122.
56. Good, "Interface," 392.
57. Goodman, "p-value fallacy," 997.
58. Yates, "Influence", 32.
59. ICH, "E9," paragraph 1.2.
60. ICH, "E9," paragraphs 2.1.2 and 3.5; Sterne and Smith, "Sifting the evidence."

34 *Paradigms for Statistical Inference*

In the experiment of Chapter 2, indirect frequentism would suggest leaving "the reader the task of deciding whether to reject"[61] H_0, as he or she brings $Pr(+T|H_0)$ and $Pr(-T|H_1)$ together with other knowledge about the object or about Attribute A.

It seems difficult to disagree with N-P, in regarding indirect frequentism as "outside the realm of the objective scientific method,"[62] because this paradigm's conclusions originate in the subjective mind of the scientist, and not in objective data. Rather than the "automatic technology" that is direct frequentism, the indirect frequentism Fisher promoted amounts to what he called an "artful science."[63]

Indirect frequentism's principal inferential result is the p that Fisher popularized. It is usually read as a "measure of evidence"[64] to be combined, somehow, with other forms of evidence about the tested hypothesis. McLean, for instance, claims that "[t]he role of statistics is to provide evidence based on observed data, hopefully very objective, and to some extent to provide an assessment of the strength of that evidence, for or against some model . . . The purpose in carrying out the test is to assess the strength of this evidence in favor of the alternative. If the evidence is strong enough, the null model is rejected."[65]

A variety of guidelines, some of them mutually conflicting, have been published for "assessing," as McLean says, the strength of evidence supposedly conveyed by p. In 1944, Fisher proposed that, "[i]f p is between *0.1* and

61. McClave and Dietrich, *Statistics*.

62. Goodman, "p-values, hypothesis tests and likelihood," 493.

63. Fisher, *Statistical Methods for Research Workers,* 9th ed.

64. Chinn, "Statistics for the European."

65. McLean, "On the nature and role," 6, 10. In light of the difficulties with measuring evidence noted in what follows, we might wonder how, as McLean says, evidence can be "provided" or "assessed" objectively.

0.9 there is certainly no reason to suspect the hypothesis tested. If it is below *0.02* it is strongly indicated that the hypothesis fails to account for the whole of the facts. We shall not often be astray if we draw a conventional line at *0.05*."[66] He amplified this line of reasoning seven years later, saying it was "usual and convenient for experimenters to take 5 per cent as a standard level of significance, in the sense that they are prepared to ignore all results which fail to reach this standard."[67]

Burdette and Gehan provided more detailed guidelines, not completely in agreement with those of Fisher, concerning using p to assess evidence against the "null" (that is, the tested) hypothesis. They suggested researchers categorize the evidence according to Table 3.1:[68]

Table 3.1: Burdette and Gehan's Suggested Characterizations of P-values

Significance Level of Data	Interpretation
Less than *1%*	Very strong evidence against the null hypothesis
1% to *5%*	Moderate evidence against the null hypothesis
5% to *10%*	Weak evidence against the null hypothesis
10% or more	Little or no real evidence against the null hypothesis

The guidelines of Fisher, Burdette and Gehan and others, despite their disagreements in many respects, have standardized interpretations of p-values to some extent.

66. Fisher, *Statistical Methods for Research Workers,* 9th ed.
67. Fisher, *Design,* 13.
68. Burdette and Gehan, *Planning and Analysis,* 9.

Nonetheless, in several respects, the indirect frequentist researcher using p to measure evidence and, thereby, evaluate hypotheses takes on a considerable amount of freedom, leading to a suspicion, at least, of mystification and arbitrariness in interpreting p. Firstly, among the scores of textbooks and papers I have surveyed that discuss p, those that suggest guidelines for gauging the evidence conveyed by p, such as the books of Fisher, and Burdette and Gehan cited thus far, do not justify their guidelines. Others provide no guidelines at all, saying at most that a smaller p signifies stronger evidence against the tested hypothesis. In fact, in 1956, Fisher even withdrew his earlier support for the conventional threshold of *0.05* or, indeed, any fixed threshold at all, for declaring results significant: "[T]he calculation is absurdly academic, for in fact no scientific worker has a fixed level of significance at which, from year to year, and in all circumstances, he rejects hypotheses; he rather gives his mind to each particular case in the light of his evidence and his ideas."[69]

Secondly, books explaining significance testing methods do not indicate the strength of evidence ("very strong," "strong," "moderate," etc.) necessary for declaring the tested hypotheses false; thus, whatever a researcher feels about the strength of the evidence, nothing ultimately obliges him to consider H true or false. Thirdly, as even its proponents agree, p cannot reflect evidence in favor of any hypothesis.[70] Therefore, whereas Popper and others would have us consider a hypothesis sufficiently supported or trustworthy when sufficiently many (or, perhaps, a sufficient proportion of) tests have failed to reject it,[71] the researcher is still at

69. Fisher, *Statistical Methods and Scientific Inference*, 41–42.

70. Fisher, *Design*, 16. However, in "Statistical methods and scientific induction," 73, he did say that by a non-significant result a hypothesis can be "confirmed or strengthened" in some unspecified way and degree.

71. Popper, "Problem of induction."

liberty to define for himself how many tests are "sufficiently many." For all these reasons, significance testing preserves "the right of other free minds to utilize [statistical results] in making their own decisions" that, as mentioned above, was so important to Fisher.

A fourth feature of indirect frequentism that lends substantial freedom to the statistician in measuring evidence is that, whereas this paradigm uses "standard statistical methods (e.g., hypothesis testing, estimation, confidence intervals)" to measure evidence, "the theory behind those methods contains no defined concept of evidence and no answer to the basic question 'When is it correct to say that a given body of data represents evidence supporting one statistical hypothesis over another?'"[72] Without a specific definition of evidence, indirect frequentists' claims to measure it signify nothing; they are neither true nor false. Statisticians can presuppose and use any number of (potentially mutually conflicting) measures of evidence (some of them outlined by Chan and Darwiche[73]), all equally indefensibly. Similarly, statisticians are in no way restrained from proposing a wide variety of disparate guidelines for characterizing p as "strong," "moderate," etc. evidence, none more or less justifiably than any others.

With different meanings of evidence in mind, frequentists could even disagree with one another as to whether the evidence from a given data set supports or undermines a hypothesis. A classic example is the difference between what might be called "absolute" and "relative" evidence. Consider testing the hypothesis H_0 which states that the mean of a particular approximately normal population is 0.[74] A random

72. Royall, "On the Probability," 760.
73. Chan and Darwiche, "On the revision," 70.
74. In general, a normal population distributes its probability in the form of what is often called a "bell-shaped" curve.

sample from the population yields a sample mean of *1* (*p= 0.0001*). For many statisticians who think of evidence as "absolute," meaning that it refers to a single hypothesis, this result would constitute strong evidence against H_0. However, other statisticians think of evidence as a tool for comparing the support for one hypothesis, relative to that for another hypothesis. If H_0 is being compared to the hypothesis H_1 stating that the mean is *3*, then these statisticians might regard the observed sample mean of *1* as evidence in favor of H_0 relative to H_1, since this sample mean is closer to *0* than to *3*.

Even the distinction between absolute and relative evidence is not sufficiently precise, however, to avoid all confusion concerning measuring evidence, at least for the reason that it does not specify whether evidence must refer to the functional, practical differences between hypotheses. For instance, perhaps population means of both *1* and *3* are high enough concentrations of a poison to kill unwanted bacteria. From a functional point of view, then, *1* and *3* are indistinguishable from each other, and both differ considerably from *0*. The relevant question here is whether, as we attempt to measure the evidence associated with the sample mean of *1*, our concept of evidence should reflect the practical equivalence of the concentrations of *1* and *3*.

Yet other statisticians interpret statistical evidence as a posterior probability.[75] The most commonly accepted definition and treatment of this evidence of which I am aware, though, is that given by the so-called "evidentialists," among whom are Royall[76] and Hacking.[77] On both philosophical and practical grounds, evidentialists reason that, given data *X=x* (which is shorthand for saying that the observed value

75. Berger and Sellke, "Testing a point null;" Casella and Berger, "Reconciling Bayesian and frequentist."
76. Royall, *Statistical Evidence*.
77. Hacking, *Logic of Statistical*.

of X is x), the measure of evidence for hypothesis H_1 vis-à-vis hypothesis H_2 is the likelihood ratio (*LR*), defined as $f(x|H_1)/f(x|H_2)$. Here, each $f(x|H_i)$ is the likelihood function of H_i. When X is a continuous variable, each f is also called the probability density function (PDF) of X assuming H_i. When X is a discrete variable, each f is also called the probability mass function of X assuming H_i. For the sake of brevity, in the following paragraphs, I will assume X is continuous, so that each f is a PDF.

If *LR* >1, then the *LR* indicates how much $X=x$ favors H_1 more than H_2, that is, the *LR* measures the strength of evidence in favor of H_1 vis-à-vis in favor of H_2. Conversely, *LR* <1 indicates how much $X=x$ favors H_2 more than H_1. The *LR* measures evidence in the sense that it indicates precisely the change, resulting from observing $X=x$, in the odds of H_1 versus H_2. In particular, multiplying the *LR* times the pre-experimental odds, $Pr(H_1) / Pr(H_2)$, yields the post-experimental odds, $Pr(H_1|x) / Pr(H_2|x)$. The evidentialist definition of evidence therefore regards evidence as relative (that is, between two explicitly defined hypotheses) but not dependent on or reflective of practical differences between hypotheses.

As mentioned above, to speak of measuring statistical evidence signifies nothing until one defines that evidence. Let us, therefore, adopt the evidentialist meaning of evidence, at least provisionally, if only because this meaning is the most widely accepted one. We would also do well to consider what we mean by saying "to measure;" the primary definition is "to ascertain the extent, dimensions, quantity, capacity, etc., of, esp. by comparison with a standard."[78] Understanding evidence and measurement in these ways, however, leads to a problem with indirect frequentists' attempts to measure evidence: The evidential strength associated with a p of any given magnitude varies with the sample

78. Random House Unabridged Dictionary, 2006.

size; in particular, any given *p* entails stronger evidence in a small trial than in a large one.[79] This is to say that taking *p* as a measure of evidence induces a type of "incoherence" in statistical inference; for example, *p=0.02* might represent stronger evidence in a small trial than *p=0.01* does in a large trial! Such a possibility presents a predicament for Burdette, Gehan, Fisher, McLean, Cohen, and the innumerable other indirect frequentists who take smaller p-values to imply stronger evidence. This dependence on sample size might help explain why Fisher's guideline above differs from that of Burdette and Gehan. It may also account for how authors do not justify their guidelines on categorizing the strength of the evidence—no justification can be given. More importantly, though, it casts serious doubt on any hopes we might have, in any particular situation, of "ascertaining the extent, dimensions [or] quantity" of evidence conceived in the evidentialist manner.

Then again, sample size is just one of many extraneous factors which complicate the interpretation of frequentist results as evidence, thereby obfuscating indirect frequentist reasoning. Another factor is the inclusion of "more extreme" values in the definition of *p*. This inclusion means that "[a] single trial in which results are 'more extreme' depends not only on the observed data, but also on the stopping rule, the number of looks at the data, and sometimes how many other comparisons were made."[80] These factors, and not only evidence, influence the value of *p* and, thereby, obscure the expression of evidence in *p*; to use *p* to assess evidence accurately, one would have to "back out" their effects from it. How this could be done is anything but clear, allowing the researcher a great deal of autonomy in interpreting *p*.

79. Royall, "Effect of sample size."
80. Goodman, "Meta-analysis."

Assessing evidence using indirect frequentist results is, in summary, a matter of states of mind, preferences, judgment and discretion. Not surprisingly, different researchers implement it in conflicting ways. But measuring the evidence from observed statistical data is only the first challenge of indirect frequentist inference. The second challenge is combining this evidence with expert knowledge and opinions; I will not discuss that process here, except to say that no firm or clear rules seem to govern it either. On the whole, therefore, it is not far off the mark to extend Neyman's comment about significance test conclusions—that they are "Delphic Pronouncements"[81] about hypotheses—to indirect frequentist inference in general.

Objective and Subjective Bayesianism

Direct and indirect frequentism, I have shown, call on the statistician to reinterpret frequencies of data given hypotheses, as if they were statements about hypotheses given data. Bayesian statistical inference, in contrast, provides explicit posterior (that is, post-analytic) inductive inferences.[82] These inferences usually take the forms of probabilities of hypotheses. In other words, bayesian statistical results are intrinsically statements about hypotheses and parameters; they require no such reinterpretations.

Bayesian inference most often makes use of Bayes' Theorem, a form of which is

$$Pr(H|x) = Pr(H) \times Pr(x|H) / Pr(x).$$

In this equation,

- $Pr(H|x)$ = the "posterior," or post-analytic probability of H given x,

---

81. Efron, "RA Fisher," 122.
82. Krams, et al., "The past is future."

- $Pr(H)$ = the "prior," or pre-analytic probability of H,
- $Pr(x|H)$ = the "likelihood," or probability of x assuming H, and
- $Pr(x)$ = the probability of x averaging over all possible hypotheses.

The above form of Bayes' Theorem can be expressed in words as, "The probability of H given x equals the prior probability of H, times the probability of x given H, divided by the probability of x." This theorem shows that, through the fraction $Pr(x|H) / Pr(x)$, x revises the pre-experimental $Pr(H)$ to yield the post-experimental $Pr(H|x)$. In particular, if $Pr(x|H) / Pr(x) > 1$, then x increases the certainty of, or confirms H; if $Pr(x|H) / Pr(x) < 1$, x decreases that certainty, disconfirming H.

Many bayesians regard Bayes' Theorem as self evident, for the reason that this theorem is a straightforward consequence—and arguably the most important known consequence[83]—of Kolmogorov's definition of conditional probability,

$$Pr(B|A) = Pr(A \text{ and } B) / Pr(A),$$

for any propositions A and B. To visualize how this definition may be used and why it seems correct, consider the act of rolling a die. Let A be the proposition {the face showing is even} and B the proposition {the face showing is less than 4}. Then, $Pr(A)=1/2$, $Pr(A \text{ and } B)=Pr(\{2\})=1/6$ and thus $Pr(B|A)=(1/6)/(1/2)=1/3$. This conclusion agrees with our expectation that, if the face showing is even, then the face showing can be less than 4 only when that face is 2 and, again conditional on the face showing being even, that face being 2 has probability $1/3$.

---

83. Stanford Encyclopedia of Philosophy, "Bayes' Theorem," Section 1.

Paradigms for Statistical Inference 43

We may also illustrate how the above form of Bayes' Theorem serves the statistician by measuring, in the experiment in Chapter 2, the posterior probability of Hypothesis H_0. The datum is $+T$ and that posterior probability is

$$Pr(H_0|+T) = 0.05Pr(H_0)/[0.05Pr(H_0)+0.80Pr(H_1)],$$

where the denominator is derived using the formula

$$Pr(+T)=Pr(+T|H_0)Pr(H_0)+Pr(+T|H_1)Pr(H_1).$$

If, say, before the experiment the (prior) probability $Pr(H_0)$ of H_0 was 90%, then the post-experimental (posterior) probability $Pr(H_0|x)$ would be 36%. The posterior probability is less than the prior probability, since $Pr(+T|H_0)/Pr(+T)<1$. Thus, the datum $+T$ decreases the certainty of H_0, agreeing with our intuition that a positive test result increases the probability $Pr(H_1)$ that the object studied has Attribute *A*.

More generally, Bayesian posterior probabilities of hypotheses may be identified by deriving posterior probability distributions of statistical parameters, using a slightly different version of Bayes' Theorem:

$$g(\theta|x) = g(\theta) \times f(x|\theta)/f(x).$$

In this equation,

- $g(\theta|x)$ = the "posterior," or post-analytic probability distribution of the statistical parameter θ ("theta") given datum x,
- $g(\theta)$ = the "prior," or pre-analytic probability distribution of θ,
- $f(x|\theta)$ = the "likelihood," or probability of x assuming θ, and
- $f(x)$ = the probability of x averaging over all possible values for θ.

Prior and posterior probability distributions, $g(\theta)$ and $g(\theta|x)$, when graphed, appear as smooth curves, series of spikes, or mixtures of curves and spikes. They support calculating probabilities of hypotheses as follows. Consider the hypothesis H that θ lies within a particular interval $[a,b]$, where a and b are any numbers such that $a \leq b$. The area under g between a and b represents the epistemic probability of H. The higher is g in the region between a and b, the greater that probability.

One building block of Bayes' Theorem, the likelihood, deserves special attention. The likelihood indicates "what the data say"[84] in the sense of expressing, for each possible parameter value or hypothesis, how well those data are predicted by that value or hypothesis. All frequentist and bayesian paradigms make some use of the likelihood, but they assign to it different roles. Direct frequentism takes areas under the likelihood over ranges of x-values to determine directly the credibility of relevant hypotheses and parameters; for instance, it reads the p-value as the probability of the tested hypothesis. Indirect frequentism tries to interpret those areas as inferential evidence that can be combined informally with prior knowledge, opinions, and so on.

In bayesianism, however, the likelihood serves to adjust pre-analytic beliefs about hypotheses and parameters, to yield post-analytic beliefs. As shown above in both $Pr(H) \times Pr(x|H)$ and $g(\theta) \times f(x|\theta)$, Bayes' Theorem prescribes precisely how to combine the likelihood with prior probabilities, specifying, in the end, the level of certainty of each hypothesis of interest. These levels of certainty are statements about hypotheses based on data, fitting well our definition above of statistical inference. Their inferential import can be grasped quite readily, for they address the inductive question, "What have I learned concerning my hypotheses from this experiment?" rather than the frequentist question, "What would happen if I repeated this experiment many

---

84. Royall, "On the Probability," 760.

Paradigms for Statistical Inference 45

times?"[85] The bayesian, then, unlike the frequentist, need not impute inferential meaning to his or her results.

Despite these apparent advantages of bayesianism, only a minority of statisticians identify themselves as bayesian[86] and, as recently as 1999, most statistics departments did not even regularly offer bayesian courses.[87] Indeed, collectively, frequentist rather than bayesian statistics is often called "the dominant school of medical statistics,"[88] "conventional statistical inference,"[89] "classical analysis,"[90] or "standard methods."[91] As noted in Chapter 1 above, significance testing "is viewed not only as chief vehicle for making *statistical* inferences, but for drawing *scientific* inferences, too."

Bayesianism's comparative lack of popularity is usually attributed to its explicit need for priors such as *Pr(H)* above: "Perhaps the most controversial aspect of [Bayes'] theorem is the use of the notion of a 'prior' probability. This concept has been severely criticized by non-bayesian statisticians as representing subjective bias."[92] *A fortiori*, "[i]f we make no assumption about prior probability, then the posterior probability can vary anywhere from 0% to 100% (not a very helpful conclusion); yet, if we choose any spe-

85. Ellison, "Statistics and science," 365.

86. Sterne, "Teaching hypothesis tests," 990. In fact, "[T]here are only 322 citations for the search string <Bayes*> among 374,747 <clinical trial> citations in the Library of Medicine's PubMed data base since the publication of Cornfield's seminal 1969 paper proposing the application of Bayes' theorem to clinical trial assessment" (Diamond and Kaul, "Prior Convictions").

87. Berger, "Bayesian analysis," Section 1.

88. Goodman, "p-value fallacy," 995.

89. Ibid, 997.

90. Diamond and Forrester, "Clinical Trials," 387; Howard, "The 2 by 2 Table," 351.

91. Berger and Berry, "Statistical analysis," 159 and 165.

92. Schaffner, "Ethically optimizing."

cific value for prior probability, we are likely to be criticized for being arbitrary in our choice. The critical limitation of bayesian analysis, therefore, centers on the issue of prior probability."[93] Thomas Bayes himself was so fearful of criticism on the point of prior probabilities that he withheld publication of his main treatise as long as he lived;[94] the work was only discovered and published by a friend two years after his death. On account of bayesianism's need for prior probabilities, Lehmann, too, argued that, while bayesian analyses allow "stronger conclusions," they also require "assumptions which are correspondingly more detailed and hence less reliable."[95]

At the same time, according to some authors, another reason frequentist methods are used more often than bayesian ones is that, through the transposition of conditioning and other re-interpretations of the usual frequentist results, researchers believe they can obtain inductive meaning while avoiding the annoying need for bayesian priors. Suggestions that psychologists, for instance, "turn bayesian fell on deaf ears, both in the United States and in Europe. Researchers had their [methods of Fisher, Neyman, and Pearson], which seemed to them the objective way to do scientific inference, whereas bayesian statistics looked subjective. And given the distorted statistical intuitions of many," specifically, of direct frequentists, "there was actually no need; the [p-value] already seemed to specify the desired bayesian posterior probabilities."[96]

Traditionally, bayesian priors are classified as either "subjective" or "objective" and, in turn, bayesians are classified as "subjective" or "objective" according to the types of priors they prefer. Subjective priors are formed using

93. Diamond and Forrester, "Clinical trials," 389.
94. Bayes, "An essay towards solving."
95. Lehmann, "Point Estimation," 2.
96. Gigerenzer, "Superego, ego," 333.

Paradigms for Statistical Inference 47

whatever background information is available about hypotheses, such as expected magnitudes of effects, findings of previous studies, professional opinions, and so forth. They could be constructed so as to reflect the degrees of beliefs of a single person, or those of a community. Not everyone agrees, though, about the admissible types of information for forming these priors, or the ways they should be combined. For example, scientific empiricists form priors based primarily on experimentation, whereas scientific rationalists emphasize introspective theorizing.[97] In any case, however, Chapter 7 below discusses in more detail two methods of forming subjective priors: elicitation and measurement of maximum betting odds. Elicitation in the above experiment, for instance, might involve asking a panel of recognized experts about the pre-experimental credibility of each of H_1 and H_0. If they can agree on a value of *1/3* for the prior *Pr(H_0)*, for instance, then the corresponding posterior probability is *Pr(H_0|+T)=0.03*. Notably, this value for *Pr(H_0|+T)* differs from the value of *0.05* that a direct frequentist, knowing that *Pr(+T|H_0)=0.05*, might infer from the transposition of conditioning. Alternatively, measurement of maximum betting odds might be used to determine *Pr(H_0)* by asking a person or people, before they have observed the test result, how much they would wager that H_0 is true.

Objective priors, in contrast to subjective ones, make no use of opinions or expert knowledge, however sincerely or firmly opinions and knowledge may be held. These priors are formed utilizing only mathematical principles, such as uniformity, "maximum entropy" and "non-informativity." A uniform prior, for instance, for the experiment above would assign 50% probability to each of H_1 and H_0; this would lead to the final inference that *Pr(H_0|+T)=0.06*. By employing these principles, objective bayesians are sometimes more

97. Geertsema, "A Christian view."

successful in reaching agreement on priors than are subjective bayesians. Different principles do, however, occasionally generate conflicting objective priors. Additionally, some critics argue that these principles are irrelevant in practical applications; it is unclear that uniformity, for instance, has anything to do, in our experiment, with pre-experimental beliefs concerning H_1 and H_0, or why uniformity should be taken as a summary of those beliefs.

In subsequent chapters, I will discuss a few of the PLI's implications concerning priors, Bayesianism and, more generally, statistical paradigms.

Summary of Paradigms for Statistical Inference

Several clarifications are appropriate at the close of this presentation of statistical paradigms. First, it must be admitted that, in some scientific fields in which statistical inference is applied, indirect frequentism has for the most part displaced direct frequentism. Some statisticians accustomed to working in those fields might claim that direct frequentism has seen its day, and is no longer appreciably influential.

There are reasons, however, for believing that, despite indirect frequentism's upsurge in popularity in some areas, direct frequentism still commands a substantial following, at least in medical applications of statistics. Salsburg, for one, claimed that medical journals will usually publish the results of studies if and only if—in direct frequentist fashion—the p-value is significant.[98]

Sterne presents empirical evidence for the continuing influence of direct frequentism.[99] He communicates the results of a survey which studied how medical schools in the

98. Salsburg, "Religion of statistics," 220.
99. Sterne, "Teaching hypothesis tests," 990.

United Kingdom teach the interpretations of significance and hypothesis test outcomes. The survey administrators requested the statistics faculty of 16 such schools to agree or disagree, on a questionnaire, with the following two statements (among other statements):

- "If P<0.05 then the difference is statistically significant and we reject the null hypothesis. If P>0.05 then we accept the null hypothesis," and

- "There are two types of error we might make: A type I error is when we reject the null hypothesis when it is in fact true. A type II error is when we do not reject the null hypothesis when it is false. In practice we reject the null hypothesis when P<0.05."

These statements are plainly direct frequentist. Fully half (eight) of the 16 schools agreed with the first, and seven agreed with the second. These numbers of votes point to a somewhat even split between direct and indirect frequentist thinking in UK medical schools and, likely, elsewhere, not to mention a lack of unanimity concerning several fundamental statistical concepts (significance, rejection and acceptance of hypotheses, and types of statistical errors). Thus, it seems likely that, while indirect frequentism may exert more influence at present than it did 50 years ago, its direct counter-pole is by no means obsolete.

More evidence of the continued influence of direct frequentism can be found in Europe's, the United States' and Japan's pharmaceutical industries. There, detailed documents called study protocols direct the conduct and statistical analyses of clinical trials. Most protocols for studies designed to demonstrate the efficacy of some new medicine over an older one include sections stipulating "criteria for a positive study." These sections are most often phrased to the effect that "The null hypothesis of no treatment difference will be tested statistically. [name of investigative treatment] will be considered efficacious if this hypothesis is rejected in favor of [name of investigative treatment], with a significance level of 0.05." That is, the hypothesis that the new drug has a positive effect is deemed credible if and only if statistical significance is attained, plainly following a direct frequentist convention.

Another clarification concerning direct frequentism and indirect frequentism is that these paradigms are, to some extent, idealizations; some frequentists do not utilize a particular frequentism in every situation, but often switch between them, or combine elements of both. Fisher, for instance, "changed, and sometimes even reversed, parts of his logic of inference."[100] When Fisher first promoted p, he campaigned for a direct frequentist strategy of deciding whether to reject the tested hypothesis by comparing p with *0.05*; this convention of *0.05* "became part of the institutionalized . . . logic."[101] In his later life, however, he suggested the two more indirect strategies of reading p as a measure of evidence, and of adjusting decision points for p ("*p<0.05,*" "*p<0.01,*" etc.) according to extra-statistical considerations.

Statisticians nowadays, too, mix direct and indirect frequentism when they pre-experimentally select their (direct) statistical decision rules according to their (indirect) speculations regarding the prior plausibility of the tested hypothesis H and what strength of evidence would, given that plausibility, be sufficient for concluding H is false. As another example of shifting between these paradigms, many scientists, having completed a statistical analysis, form their personal beliefs by (indirectly) combining test results with their own "states of mind," and so forth, even as they submit these results to public scrutiny by appealing (directly)

---

100. Gigerenzer, "Superego, ego," 316.
101. Ibid.

to widely accepted decision rules (such as "*p<0.05*") for evaluating hypotheses.

There is yet another common way that some statisticians merge direct frequentist practices with indirect frequentist ones. On the one hand, they claim to measure evidence using p-values accurately and objectively. On the other hand, they leave evidence itself undefined and allow other scientists reviewing their results considerable autonomy in how they combine that supposedly measured evidence together with non-statistical information. McLean opines this way, asserting

> [the p-value's] most important feature is that its scale is universally acceptable. A p-value of *0.02*, say, can validly be interpreted as indicating a significant difference between the null and alternative values regardless of the distribution used ... A low p-value means that the evidence is strong; a high value means it is weak. It is legitimate to compare the results of two tests using different statistics, and say one reflects stronger evidence than the other.[102]

In short, *p* is allegedly "a measure of inductive evidence against H_0, and the smaller the value, the greater the evidence."[103] This claim is a variation of what Cornfield called the "alpha postulate."[104] It cannot be correct (at least if we define evidence in the evidentialist way) since, as I mentioned in the section above on indirect frequentism, the evidential strength associated with a *p* of any given magnitude depends on the sample size, and not only that magnitude.[105]

102. McLean, "On the nature and role," 11.

103. Hubbard and Armstrong, "Why we don't know."

104. Royall, "The effect of sample size," 313; Sterne, "Teaching hypothesis tests," 991 Item 3.

105. Even some who recognize that sample size affects the

Furthermore, a similar problem related to sample sizes plagues interpreting N-P hypothesis test results as evidence, in that any given such result conveys stronger evidence in a large trial than in a small one. Thus, sample size exerts an effect on the evidential meanings of hypothesis test results that is opposite its effect on that of p. However, it is beside the fact that neither p-values nor hypothesis test results reflect strengths of evidence accurately. When tracing the intermixing of direct frequentism and indirect frequentism, the important truth to appreciate concerning these attempts to measure evidence using frequentist results is that they represent efforts to inject a little more objectivity into the highly subjective enterprise that is indirect frequentist inference. If successful, this "hybrid" method would afford the statistical analyst the chance to appear objective, while nonetheless reserving for the consumers of his analyses the latitude of combining statistical results with other information in whatever way that suits them.

One more comment is in order about the types of frequentism identified in this chapter. Direct frequentism is not to be identified strictly with N-P's hypothesis testing and "inductive behavior," nor is indirect frequentism the same as using Fisher's p. These paradigms differ not so much in the kinds of statistical procedures used, as in whether the results of those procedures are viewed as providing final and decisive meaning concerning hypotheses. Direct frequentist inference interprets these results as unmediated, unequivocal decision functions or probabilities of hypoth-

---

evidentialist evidence associated with any particular p, thereby recognizing the alpha postulate as incorrect, misunderstand the effect of sample size on this evidence. For example, Peto et al., "Design and Analysis," and Lee, *Survival*, 334 each claims that the evidence associated with a given p is stronger in a large study than it is in a small study. This is the opposite of the truth, if evidence is defined in the evidentialist manner.

eses, whereas indirect frequentism interprets them as evidence to be combined, loosely and freely, with background information. Indeed, p is often read in direct frequentist fashion, as a probability of H; conversely, the rejection or non-rejection of H can be read indirectly merely as evidence about H_0. These paradigms differ, then, not in their mathematical procedures, but in the inferential meanings (in particular, the prescriptive-ness) they imagine the results of those procedures to convey.

Each of the four statistical paradigms I have described is a theory concerning how to answer the central inferential question identified above. Direct frequentism claims that deductive frequencies of data directly indicate inferential certainties about hypotheses. Indirect frequentism allows individual scientists to decide for themselves what those same frequencies indicate concerning hypotheses. Bayesianism expresses inferential certainties directly and precisely, in terms of probabilities of hypotheses; these certainties are derived by updating pre-experimental probabilities of hypotheses using data and mathematical principles. The subjective and objective versions of Bayesianism differ, though, with respect to how pre-experimental certainties are established—subjective bayesianism generates them using whatever information, impressions, and opinions that may be available, whereas objective bayesianism presumes they must be founded wholly on mathematical principles.

For the last century or so, statisticians and philosophers of statistics have debated actively which, if any, of these paradigms are useful, justified, correct, and reasonable, in both practical and foundational respects. As I show below, however, the Philosophy of the Law Idea (PLI) identifies some ways that particular Christian and humanist religious beliefs control which of statistical paradigms may seem acceptable.

4

The Philosophy of the Law Idea (PLI)— A Summary

THE PLI is a Christian philosophy worked out by such Dutch Calvinist thinkers as Herman Dooyeweerd and Dirk Vollenhoven. It examines relations between religious beliefs and scientific theorizing. Dooyeweerd has propounded this philosophy in the most detail, particularly in his landmark four-volume *A New Critique of Theoretical Thought*.[1] The PLI claims that all theorizing is controlled by underlying presuppositions that themselves have religious roots.

As the PLI develops the notion of the religious control of scientific theories, it pays particular attention to how these theories may be evaluated in light of Christian belief. That evaluation process is not motivated, however, by what Clouser calls the "encyclopedic assumption," the assumption that Scripture is

> an encyclopedia in which we may look for an answer to any sort of question we may have. The encyclopedic assumption may not go so far as to think that the answer to every question is in Scripture, but it does suppose Scripture to contain answers to all sorts of nonreligious questions. It ignores the Bible's own central theme

1. Dooyeweerd, *New Critique*.

and purpose, and instead of trying to ascertain the literal meaning of the text (where "literal" means the intent of the author), it tries to force the text to yield truths about matters which never crossed the minds of its author(s).[2]

The encyclopedic assumption is misdirected and wrong, holds the PLI, because people must come to God and His written word willing to listen to what God wants them to know, rather than merely what they want that word to say. Scripture addresses the topics God decreed it would address, and not necessarily the ones that humans may wish to know about. We must, then, read holy writ as it was intended to be read. Plainly, however, if a person demands that religious beliefs inform every possible investigation or decision, then he or she is apt to read into Scripture meanings that Scripture does not mean to convey.

The PLI admits, then, that the Christian Bible, for example, does not provide specific truths about many, or perhaps even most, scientific fields. Consequently, it does not promote trying to find in the Bible hints about every scientific concept whatever. As I will explain, it focuses instead on another, less direct (but nonetheless pivotal) manner in which religious beliefs influence scientific theorizing. Specifically, any religious belief delimits ranges of so-called "overviews of reality" that will look plausible to someone having that belief. An overview of reality, likewise, causes some scientific theories to seem plausible, and others to seem implausible.

The most important premise of the PLI is that all of "reality is created by God whose will is the sovereign and redeeming law for reality."[3] It claims, therefore, that whereas all scientific pursuits, Christian and otherwise, are grounded

2. Clouser, "Genesis."
3. Kalsbeek, "Introduction," 31.

on underlying religious presuppositions, Christians who are scientists must align their scientific endeavors with God's sovereign rule. To this end, the PLI further develops the idea of religious control of science by introducing and analyzing various overviews of reality. It studies how these overviews fit into the limits established by particular religious beliefs, as well as how they establish limits for science. An important outcome of the PLI's thinking in this regard is the overview of reality it proposes; in what follows, I will present some reasons to agree with the PLI that this overview is regulated by the Biblical doctrine of creation.

The Religious Control of Science

Any discussion of the relations between religious beliefs and science must assume some definition of these beliefs. To decide upon its own definition, the PLI draws from the Christian Bible and the writings of the Protestant Reformers. It also surveys a wide variety of beliefs commonly called religious, isolating what they all hold in common. It considers the characteristics shared by all beliefs considered religious, and the characteristics of religious beliefs that distinguish them from other beliefs.

As a consequence of these investigations, the PLI identifies a belief as religious if the belief involves what is regarded as divine, where divinity itself is equivalent to self-existence or self-sufficiency. That is, religious beliefs concern whatever is thought not to depend on anything else for its existence or meaning.[4] Beliefs both about what is thought to be divine, and about how the divine is thought to relate to the non-divine, are religious.

Christians, in particular, share the religious belief that only God is self-existent; all else—"things in heaven and

---

4. Clouser, *Myth,* 1st ed, 21.

on earth, visible and invisible"[5]—was created by Christ and for Christ. Everything (in the most inclusive sense possible) besides God depends on Him, for both its coming into being and its continuing to be. Christians believe, further, that nothing besides God is self-sufficient, for in Christ "all things hold together."[6] Calvin condensed these two thrusts of Scripture by declaring "[t]here is nothing so proper to God as eternity and self-existence."[7]

On the other hand, another belief system widely referred to as humanism maintains that one or a few elements or features of humanness, such as free will or logical thought, are the essence of humans. It goes on to suppose these elements are self-existent or self-sufficient. Humanism can, therefore, be recognized not only as religious, but also as incompatible with Christian beliefs. I will explain more about humanism below.

Defining religious beliefs as beliefs about the self-existent and self-sufficient, the PLI examines the ways they provide foundations for what have traditionally been called "overviews of reality" or "general theories of reality."[8] Any such overview "is a theory that tries to discover the essential nature of reality. Its aim may be stated as trying to find what kinds of things are there."[9] It provides an explanation for the general relations and connections between the ways we experience reality, that is, between the numerous aspects, or types of properties and laws, possessed by concrete things. In simple terms, "if the various aspects of the things we experi-

---

5. Col 1:16.
6. Col 1:17.
7. Calvin, *Institutes*, I, xiv, 3.
8. Clouser, *Myth*, 1st ed, 70
9. Clouser, *Myth*, 2nd ed, 71.

ence are represented as beads on a necklace, then a general theory of reality wants to know, 'What is the string?'"[10]

We can further clarify overviews of reality by comparing them to scientific theories. These theories make statements about the properties and laws of a particular type; for instance, theories in physics seek to identify properties and laws of the physical type, and mathematical theories deal with quantitative properties and laws. An overview of reality, in contrast, investigates how each type of property and law relates to the other types of properties and laws.

The primary way a person's religious beliefs delimit his or her overviews of reality may be obvious at this point: Whatever someone views as self-existent and self-sufficient determines a range of acceptable explanations concerning how the aspects relate to one another. For instance, once a humanist holds the religious belief that one or more elements of humanness are divine, he or she is bound to elevate those elements to a more important or more basic status in his or her overview of reality.

Overviews of reality impact science in several ways. First, they determine what sorts of arguments scientists consider to be sound. For instance, a mathematician who believes (as did Leibniz, among others) that the only important or real properties and laws are quantitative ones will tend to ignore, discredit, or downplay any conclusions of a scientific study besides empirical measurements and quantitative reasoning based on such measurements. Second, these overviews set limits for science by influencing our standpoints on how specific fields of study relate to other such fields and other types of properties and laws. Ernst Mach, for example, for whom the speed of sound has been named, held that all of human experience is nothing

---

10. Ibid.

but sensory perceptions and feelings.[11] If Mach was correct, then even after perceiving something, one can never know whether that thing possesses any physical properties.

On a practical level, overviews of reality "make us more likely to notice certain features of things, alter what we see as important, and determine both the questions we ask and which hypotheses will look acceptable as answers to them."[12] The PLI studies these effects of overviews on scientific theorizing in some detail. Its central claim about these effects matters the most to us, however, and can be summarized as follows: Religious beliefs set the limits within which overviews of reality will seem plausible and, subsequently, these overviews set analogous limits for theories. In this way, these beliefs "regulate or guide the way people think."[13] Alternatively, to make the same point in reverse order, "scientific theories necessarily presuppose an overview of reality, while overviews of reality necessarily presuppose some *per se* divinity belief."[14] This conception of the indirect influence of religious beliefs on science accounts for "the general Biblical view that no one understands creation who does not know its Creator,"[15] while nonetheless avoiding the (untenable) encyclopedic assumption.

Admittedly, most scientists only tacitly assume their religious beliefs and, especially, their overviews of reality; they do not usually discuss their own or anyone else's, and may never even become conscious of them.[16] In any theorizing, though, "there is always an influence of a metaphysical belief whether or not a scientist is conscious of it or has ever

11. Encyclopædia Britannica, *Ernest Mach*, 2007.
12. Clouser, *Myth*, 1st ed, 167.
13. Clouser, *Myth*, 2nd ed, 123.
14. Ibid, 78.
15. Clouser, "Replies," 26.
16. Clouser, *Myth*, 1st ed, 61.

been exposed to its formal exposition in a theory."[17] Whether or not we are at all explicit about religious beliefs, through our overviews of reality, they impact our scientific activities. This progression from religious beliefs to overviews to theories applies to all theories, whether controlled by Christian or non-Christian beliefs; in an indirect yet critical sense, then, every scientific endeavor rests on a religious foundation.

In the next subsections, I describe the PLI's Biblically-consistent overview of reality, both illustrating how an overview can fit into the bounds set by Christian beliefs, and laying some groundwork for assessing how consistent is each of the above statistical paradigms with Christian belief. I also go over the main points of the PLI's analysis of humanist religious beliefs, and overviews of reality consistent with these beliefs, which were dominant in Western Culture when some of the above statistical paradigms were introduced and became popular. This review of humanism and its associated overviews will prepare us to identify points of agreement between them and statistical paradigms.

Aspectual Irreducibility

The PLI sets forth an overview of reality in which reality displays itself in fifteen or so "aspects," or kinds of properties and laws: quantitative, spatial, kinematic, physical, biological, sensory (feeling), logical, historical, linguistic, social, economic, aesthetic, jural, ethical, and fiduciary.[18] The order of this list is important, in that active functioning in any aspect presupposes active functioning in all the aspects earlier in the list.[19]

17. Clouser, "General Relation."
18. Dooyeweerd, *Roots*, 33.
19. Clouser, *Myth*, 1st edition, 209; functioning in an aspect refers to the way a thing possesses properties and/or is subject to laws of that aspect.

While most of these aspects are fairly self-explanatory, I do need to say a few words here about the fiduciary aspect in particular. Fiduciary properties and laws have to do with the certainty of propositions, the confidence and beliefs we might have in them, and the trust we might place in a person or thing. They therefore comprise a primary focus of statistical inference. Other aspects of particular interest to statistical inference are the quantitative and logical aspects. We might, in fact, re-phrase the central question of statistical inference stated in Chapter 2 in terms of these aspects, saying that this inference's primary task is to measure the *quantitative* degrees of *fiduciary* certainties of *logical* hypotheses.

According to Colossians 1 (as noted above), each aspect is created by God (rather than divine) and depends directly on Him for its continued existence. The PLI infers from this universal created-ness that each aspect is equally important and real. Another way of saying this is that all the aspects have identical ontological status. Thus, we may not regard any aspect as that which has generated other parts of reality, such as other aspects. Doing so would confer God's creatorship upon that aspect, making it a substitute creator and, thus, an idol. We may not consider *kinematic* movement, for example, as only an infinite series of discrete *spatial* magnitudes,[20] or mathematics, which focuses on the *quantitative* aspect, as nothing but a *logical* process.[21] Similarly, we may not adopt the materialism of Karl Marx, which presupposes that "matter/energy is the basic reality; . . . physical matter . . . is 'just there.' Matter depends on nothing whatever, and all of reality either is identical with or depends on matter."[22] That materialism

---

20. Dooyeweerd, *New Critique*, II, 103.
21. Ibid, 82.
22. Clouser, *Myth*, 2nd ed, 46.

presumes everything either is or is produced by purely physical realities.

The philosophical term for putting forward any part of creation as that which generates or makes possible the rest is "reduction." The PLI insists that Christians should take a non-reductive view of all topics because, when a view, such as Marx's materialism, regards something created as "more real" or "more basic" than other things, reducing them to it, the view treats that thing as divine (This refers only to ontological reduction. What some philosophers have called "supervenience," to designate an order of appearance of certain kinds of properties, is unobjectionable[23]).

Many Christians have, nonetheless, regarded scientific theories acceptable that reduce some aspects to others, so long as the reducing aspects are said to depend likewise upon God.[24] The PLI objects to that practice, however. For, elevating any aspects above others is at odds with the way Bible writers always speak of all creation depending intimately and directly on God, and with the teaching that only Christ mediates God's sustaining power to creation.[25]

One might agree that no part of the universe exists independently or causes the existence of other parts and, yet, hold that some parts can be *understood* completely in terms of other parts. In particular, it might be suggested that, by investigating the properties of a thing within just one or two aspects, one can grasp the properties of that thing within other aspects. A wedge is thus introduced between the existence of something and its meaning, so that even though no concrete thing is divine or semi-divine, some types of meaning may be so. However, standing against such reductions is the basic truth that God created "all things, visible or invis-

23. Ibid, 359–60.
24. Clouser, *Myth*, 1st ed, 172.
25. Col 1:15. See also Calvin, *Institutes*, I, xiii.

ible," including all meaning.[26] Reducing types of meaning to other types is therefore as misguided as is attributing the existence of some created things to that of others.

A possible misunderstanding needs to be avoided: One might contend that I myself am being reductive, by reducing things to their religious meanings. This claim, though, very likely reflects a view, found in scholasticism and also popular elsewhere, that in everything there are two sides, the "sacred" and the "secular," or "grace and nature." This belief has its roots in Ancient Greek philosophy. I cannot deal here with this belief in depth, except to state that God calls men and women to bring every area of human experience into deliberate obedience to His will. There is no "secular" element of creation, and to call all of reality fundamentally religious, as I have done, is not a reduction. Dooyeweerd has dealt in depth with the "sacred/secular" conception of reality.[27]

Inter-Aspectual Coherence

Not only are the aspects mentioned above mutually irreducible, they also cohere with each other, which means that

> the aspects cannot be isolated from one another; their very intelligibility depends on their connectedness. Though they may be abstracted from the things which exhibit them, they cannot—even in thought—be isolated from one another. So even though the meanings of "quantitative," "physical," "sensory," "justitial," etc., are all importantly distinct and irreducible,

---

26. Clouser, *Myth*, 1st ed, 176 ff.
27. Dooyeweerd, *Roots*.

> they can only be understood in connection with,
> and by being compared to, one another.[28]

Because of this coherence, each science can convey meaning when it recognizes, refers to and explicates a multiplicity of aspects: "No matter how hard a science may try to exclude all but its delimiting aspect, it cannot avoid dealing with the [properties] its data display in the other aspects."[29]

The irreducibility and coherence between the aspects imply general principles for the statistical task of assessing quantitative degrees of fiduciary certainty of logical hypotheses. Because of irreducibility, statistics must not try to derive certainties about scientific hypotheses solely from quantitative data. Because of inter-aspectual coherence, statistics must respect the connections between the aspects, especially between the quantitative, logical, and fiduciary aspects ones. In Chapters 5 through 8, I will investigate some of what these principles entail for various statistical paradigms.

The PLI and Humanism

In the sixteenth and early seventeenth centuries, Western thought by and large proceeded under the influences of

> the Greeks through logic, mathematics, etc. and [of] the Judaeo-Christian heritage with its teaching of a supreme God who created and continues to uphold all things . . . By the middle of the eighteenth century [however] under the influence of Immanuel Kant, the separation of science and faith was complete . . . [T]his pretended separation was not a giving up on faith but rather replacing faith in God as creator with the humanistic faith in man—the arbiter of all

28. Clouser, *Myth*, 1st ed, 217.
29. Ibid.

things . . . Early in the nineteenth century the
Romantic movement was in full swing with its
emphasis on the individual and [his or her]
feelings.[30]

Based on its analysis of these historical developments, the PLI identifies the major "religious ground-motives" guiding Western culture, including this culture's sciences.[31] Among these motives is humanism which, as noted above, supposes that one or a few of the aspects of humanness mentioned above are the essence of humans. It regards these aspects as independent from God and every other authority, as self-sufficient and, therefore, as divine.

Humanism manifests itself in two opposing ideals, or poles: personality (freedom) and nature (science, or control).[32] The personality ideal is expressed succinctly in Jean-Jacques Rousseau's principle that each person need be obedient only to himself. It gained prominence in Western culture when, "[p]roudly conscious of his autonomy and freedom, modern man saw 'nature' as an expansive arena for the explorations of his free personality, as a field of infinite possibilities in which the sovereignty of human personality must be revealed."[33] In this ideal, "[h]umanism yields to an aesthetic enjoyment of the 'creating freedom' which reveals itself in nature."[34] That freedom derives from some feature of humanness such as reason, aesthetics, emotion, or free-will, each of which, in its turn, is viewed as divine. The personality ideal stresses the relevance of the individual's emotions, impressions, and preferences over and against universal theories and objective facts. Even if objective,

30. Satherley, "Creation and the redemption," Paragraph 3.
31. Dooyeweerd, *Roots*, 15.
32. Ibid., 149.
33. Ibid., 150 and 319.
34. Dooyeweerd, *New Critique*, I, 193.

detached reality exists, to this humanistic ideal the most important scientific truths are private and personal.

On the other hand, the nature ideal arose with René Descartes, Thomas Hobbes, and others of their time, and came to the fore in the Enlightenment.[35] Descartes conceptualized God as "pure mathematical thought," thereby setting a pattern for later science seeking its "Archimedean point," or sure anchor of certainty, in the assumed self-existence and, therefore, divinity, of quantitative reasoning.[36] Similarly, Galileo "claimed that the language of nature is written in mathematical symbols, and Alexander Pope assessed the significance of Newton's Principia (1686) with his well-known appreciation: 'Nature and Nature's laws hid in night: God said: Let Newton be! And all was light.'"[37] More generally, "[a] humanistic faith in the omnipotence of the modern science of nature dominated Western culture. The Enlightenment ideal was to control reality by discovering the laws of nature. It was assumed that such control was possible because natural laws determined the course of events in a closed chain of cause and effect . . . The creation motive of the Christian religion gave way to faith in the creative power of scientific thought which seeks its ground of certainty only within itself."[38] Emboldened by this newfound faith in quantitative thought, the Enlightenment thinkers declared confidently that the ancient Stoics' "golden age" of unmitigated happiness "is transformed from dream into blueprint, and shifts from paradise lost to paradise regained."[39]

---

35. Gay, *Enlightenment*, 17.
36. Dooyeweerd, *New Critique*, I, 193 and 196.
37. Strauss, *Paradigms*, Preface.
38. Dooyeweerd, *New Critique*, I, 106, 151 and 170.
39. Goudzwaard, *Capitalism and Progress*, 47.

Thus, although the personality and nature ideals both presupposed the self-sufficiency of humanness, they followed that presupposition with differing philosophical reductions and, hence, reached opposing conclusions concerning man's place in the world. This opposition precipitated an irreconcilable practical conflict between these ideals, even as early as the stormy encounters between Descartes and Hobbes around 1600–1650: "But it was precisely when men first entertained the new science ideal seriously that great difficulties arose. When it became apparent that science *determined* all of reality as a flawless chain of cause and effect, it was clear that nothing in reality offered a place for human *freedom*. Nature and freedom, science ideal and personality ideal—they became enemies."[40] No escape from that conflict has presented itself, because these ideals are each religious and non-negotiable, alternatively driving "the stance and world view of humanism from one pole to the other."[41] Consequently, these ideals have persisted into the twenty-first century, setting limits within which, as I will show, certain overviews of reality appear acceptable.

---

40. Dooyeweerd, *Roots*, 153.
41. Ibid, 152.

5

The Nature Ideal, Mathematicism, and Statistical Inference

Every science defines for itself, even if implicitly, a field of inquiry, which involves selecting the aspects—the kinds of properties and laws—about which it will theorize and the kinds of questions it will seek to answer about those aspects. Once a science delimits such a field, it must also at least assume ways in which those aspects relate both to each other, and to the aspects outside of its focus:

> The professional physicist, for instance, needs a notion of the modal aspect in which the phenomena of energy to be investigated present themselves. He also has to have a notion of the relation of physics to the aspects of number, space, and motion if he wants to practice his profession on a mathematical foundation. Without such a notion he would always run the risk of transgressing the boundaries of his special science. He would be guilty of confusing these boundaries, which is deemed to be an unforgivable error for the expert.[1]

---

1. Dooyeweerd, *Reformation and Scholasticism*, Chapter 3.

The central question of statistical inference identified in Chapter 2 highlights this inference's concentration on the quantitative, fiduciary, and logical aspects. Any statistically inferential statement about the degree of certainty concerning a hypothesis must, then, assume some relation between these three aspects. In this way, the PLI directs our attention unequivocally to an important and, perhaps, the most important way religious beliefs control statistical theorizing: these beliefs regulate the relations one's overview of reality posits between these aspects and, subsequently, these relations determine limits for statistical paradigms. Thus, as I discuss overviews of reality in what follows, and seek to identify points of agreement and disagreement between them and statistical paradigms, I will state, as precisely as I can, what these overviews allege and what these paradigms assume about the fiduciary, logical, and quantitative aspects.

Humanism's nature ideal proclaims humans' facility of quantitative thought as self-sufficient and, therefore, divine. It puts forward that facility as a kind of gospel, a universal method of bringing natural laws to light, controlling nature and, thereby, demonstrating the sovereignty of humans over nature and their own destiny. This ideal thereby sets bounds in which a particular overview of reality seems acceptable: a "mathematicism," as it were, which reduces human experience to quantitative laws and properties. All non-quantitative laws and properties, according to this overview, are seen as either the same as quantitative ones or as generated by them. Mathematical reasoning is, then, alleged to be uniquely qualified to determine scientific conclusions, including the levels of certainty that statistical inference attempts to derive about hypotheses. Any such reduction of fiduciary properties and laws to quantitative ones cannot, however, be justified from a mathematical point of view; for, the relations between the aspects are in the domain of philosophy, rather than of any science such as mathematics.

The PLI opposes any attempt to establish science solely on quantitative properties and laws or, more generally, solely on the properties and laws of any single aspect. It insists science must be founded instead on what it calls the "attitude of naïve thought"[2] or "prescientific" experience.[3] In this experience, we come into contact with each concrete thing as it is, *viz.*, as a multi-aspectual whole; we do not pay attention to or even notice any aspects the thing displays, to the exclusion of others: "[O]nly naïve experience sees reality in the structure it gives itself, because its attitude of thought is still fully attuned to this reality."[4] For science to harmonize with the PLI's overview of reality, then, it must take as its starting place the prescientific, rather than any single aspect. In separate work, I have dealt with prescientific experience as the necessary foundation for statistical inference in particular.[5] In Chapter 7 below, I will say more about the differences between the scientific and prescientific modes of experience.

The mark of mathematicisim in science is a regard of quantitative thought as the definitive "stamp of legitimacy"[6] for theorizing. This type of reductionism divides human experience into "human consciousness in its psychic and logical aspects" on the one hand, "and a 'reality-by-itself' in its pre-psychic and pre-logical aspects"[7] on the other hand. In other words, it carves up reality into two realms: a subjective realm of opinions, beliefs, feelings, and judgments,

2. Ibid.
3. Runner, *Relation of the Bible.*
4. Dooyeweerd, *Reformation and Scholasticism*, Chapter 3.
5. Hartley, "Philosophy of law idea and role."
6. Goodman, "p-value fallacy," 1002.
7. Dooyeweerd, *Reformation and Scholasticism*, Chapter 3.

The Nature Ideal, Mathematicism, and Statistical Inference 71

and an objective, "scientific" realm of empirical quantitative observations and the mathematical laws that may be applied to them. Only the quantitative observations and reasoning are deemed scientifically relevant. To the degree that any scientific argument is "tainted" by dependence on opinions, intuition, judgment, and so forth, this mathematicism brands it as invalid and unreliable. As noted by AWF Edwards, many medical researchers, for example, habitually form conclusions using frequentist test results alone, *sans* biological or medical knowledge.[8] Nevertheless, Edwards' reprimand speaks to mathematicism not only in medical science, but wherever it appears: "What used to be called judgment is now called prejudice."

We have reviewed two statistical paradigms that appear acceptable in the light of the mathematicist overview of reality: direct frequentism and objective bayesianism. As explained above, direct frequentism interprets the frequencies of data resulting from significance tests and hypothesis tests as direct statements of the credibility and trustworthiness of hypotheses. It also interprets maximum likelihood estimates as the best estimates of unknown statistical parameters. Both of these interpretations construe purely mathematical statements about data given hypotheses as fiduciary statements about hypotheses given data, in ways that are not themselves mathematically justified or even supported. It is difficult, therefore, to visualize direct frequentism achieving so widespread an influence, without the regulation of some type of mathematicist overview.

The protocols of pharmaceutical clinical trials mentioned in Chapter 3, for instance, often involve themselves in this mathematicism. Many of them dictate that the hypothesis that the new, investigative medication is more efficacious than the old will be considered credible or trust-

---

8. Edwards, *Likelihood*.

worthy only if the null hypothesis is rejected. Fiduciary meaning in these trials is said, then, to depend solely on the purely logical-quantitative determination that is conventional statistical significance. Revealing a direct frequentist standpoint about the valid grounds for scientific conclusions, observed data within these trials are considered to reflect real underlying population effects if and only if they are statistically significant.

Objective bayesianism, on the other hand, constructs prior probability distributions for parameters using mathematical principles such as uniformity or maximum entropy. It does not make clear why one should rely on these principles, rather than on discipline-specific pre-experimental information related to statistical parameters, to specify what to believe about those parameters before the analysis. It dogmatically takes abstract mathematical expressions, but not scientists' opinions or expectations, to be trustworthy in forming priors.

Both direct frequentism and objective bayesianism fit within the limits of the mathematicism I have described, because they try to found statistical inference exclusively on mathematical principles and quantitative experimental data, rather than on the prescientific. In the PLI's language, they start "with theoretical thought as a self-sufficient datum. This is based on its dogma regarding the autonomy of theoretic reason."[9] These paradigms claim, in the name of objectivity, that what may be concluded about hypotheses follows directly from mathematically processed empirical observations. They suppose that purging statistics of nonquantitative "subjective" elements is both possible and necessary. They insist that, without these elements, mathematically manipulated data can and must determine post-experimental quantitative levels of fiduciary certainty about

---

9. Dooyeweerd, *Reformation and Scholasticism*, Chapter 3.

statistical hypotheses. In these ways, these paradigms reduce fiduciary functioning to quantitative functioning, presupposing that fiduciary properties and laws are, or should be, generated from quantitative ones.

We have seen, then, how humanism's nature ideal allows a kind of mathematicism to seem plausible as an overview of reality. This overview, in turn, allows direct frequentism and objective bayesianism to seem plausible as statistical paradigms. Admittedly, perhaps religious beliefs other than the nature ideal could have set limits leading to the popularity of these paradigms. Establishing a *causal* link from this ideal to statistical paradigms may, therefore, be impossible, and is in any case beyond the scope of this book. Nonetheless, in view of these paradigms' peculiar tendencies, we can conclude that this ideal was instrumental in affording an intellectual environment in which the paradigms could flourish. Large numbers of statisticians and other scientists placed their trust in these paradigms because they had first placed their trust in, and given themselves over to, the nature ideal.

6

The Personality Ideal, Subjectivism, and Statistical Inference

While exclusive trust in mathematical reasoning fits into the bounds set by the humanistic nature ideal, an overview we might call "subjectivism" fits into the bounds set by humanism's personality ideal. The personality ideal makes plausible both the "autonomous freedom of the human personality" subjectivism posits "in the utterly individual disposition and genius of each person,"[1] and subjectivism's claim that nature is "a field of infinite possibilities in which the sovereignty of human personality must be revealed."[2]

The dilemma between objectivism and subjectivism "can best be understood as a controversy between contrary answers to the question, 'What is the source of the laws that give orderliness to creation?' Objectivism locates the source of order in the objects of human experience, but subjectivism locates the order in the mind of the knowing subject."[3] Subjectivism declares, along with Immanuel Kant, that the "chaotic . . . sensory-psychical impressions which form only

1. Dooyeweerd, *Roots*, 179.
2. Ibid, 150 and 319.
3. Clouser, *Myth*, 1st ed, 247.

The Personality Ideal, Subjectivism, and Statistical Inference 75

the 'material' or 'stuff' of our experience"[4]... "are fed into the mind," and the mind then "orders them into an intelligible experience."[5] Subjectivism might, therefore, be viewed as a type of the "lawlessness" in which, according to the Christian Bible, sin manifests itself.[6]

The statistical paradigm I have called "indirect frequentism" is undeniably consistent with this subjectivism. As shown in Chapter 3 above, this statistical paradigm allows humans to exercise final and sovereign judgment in evaluating abstract statistical outcomes. Indirect frequentists fabricate inductive meaning from the results of frequentist tests and ML estimation, through a speculative over-extension of sensory feeling, informally combining those results with other information to create their own personal meanings. In their own words, they independently "decide by how much a theoretical proposition has been advanced by the data,"[7] by drawing on "intuition" and mystical "states of mind,"[8] rather than on mathematical rules.

In the section in Chapter 3 on indirect frequentism, I noted several features of indirect frequentism that, collectively, afford the statistician a great deal of freedom; these features help this paradigm conform well to a subjectivist mind-set. The multiplicity of guidelines available for characterizing p as "strong," "moderate," etc. evidence permits the statistician to choose the rule that suits him or her best. Furthermore, the fact that texts and papers present only guidelines (if they even present any interpretive aids at all), and not rigid rules, for characterizing p allows the statistician

4. Ibid., 42.
5. Ibid., 208.
6. 1 Jn 3:9.
7. Cohen, "Things I have learned."
8. Good, "Interface," 392.

to characterize p using no rule at all. The unacceptability or, at least, gaucheness, of using p (or other frequentist tools) to measure evidence in support of any hypothesis licenses the indirect frequentist to decide whether a hypothesis has been tested enough, and not rejected too much, to be trustworthy. This unacceptability both prevents and excuses him from developing or following any system—methodology, if you will—as he accepts hypotheses. Most importantly, though, the lack of any definition of evidence in indirect frequentism makes measuring evidence an ambiguous idea at best, and at worst, a manipulative tool that can be wielded to the researcher's advantage.

All these subjective elements of discerning evidence from frequentist results have been noted for many years; in fact, some have been widely publicized and well known since before the 1950s.[9] Consequently, even some indirect frequentists sometimes admit the non-systematic nature of their ways of transforming their deductive frequencies of data into inductive inferences. These concessions by no means amount to acknowledgments of weakness, however; for, transcending them is a conviction, noted above and fully in line with subjectivism, that the mind can nonetheless order the "chaotic sensory-psychical impressions" that are statistical test results "into an intelligible experience." Scientists have a right, after all, said Fisher, to utilize statistical results in making "their own decisions."[10] In short, indirect frequentism lets the individual scientist be the ultimate authority and have the last word concerning the credibility of a hypothesis. This paradigm thereby satisfies the bounds set by the subjectivist overview of reality.

Now, the PLI affirms, along with subjectivism, that feelings, emotions, states of mind, and so forth, as sensory

9. Thompson, "Four Hundred Two Citations."
10. Fisher, *Statistical Methods and Scientific Induction*, 77.

functions, are indeed essential in statistically determining the credibility of a hypothesis: "It is impossible for these other aspects not to enter the explanations of each science... [A]spects cannot be isolated from one another; their very intelligibility depends on their connectedness."[11] As shown in the section in Chapter 3 on bayesianism, once data have been collected and modeled, only certain post-experimental degrees of belief are compatible with pre-experimental beliefs—some of which may be manifested in feelings and so forth—and with the accepted definition of conditional probability.

Indirect frequentism, however, "absolutizes" the role of those subjective elements in forming fiduciary beliefs about hypotheses, playing down or even denying the (equally essential) links between those beliefs and quantitative laws. It divorces the credibility of hypotheses from the logically and quantitatively normative implications of data. It takes degrees of belief to be subject to states of feeling, but not to logical and quantitative laws, denying the PLI's finding that all things are subject to the laws of all aspects all the time.[12] The resultant reduction of statistical meaning to sensory functioning, like any other aspectual reduction, "is necessarily directed to the *speciality* of meaning, which is thereby dissociated from its temporal *coherence*, and consequently becomes *meaningless* and *void*."[13] Such a splintering of the various types of properties and laws is not unlike the failure, noticed by Strauss, of certain postmodern philosophers to "develop the positive side of their critique by exploring the indubitable interaction between philosophy and the natural sciences."[14] Indirect frequentism's depreciation of mathematical and logical laws is necessarily reductive, for it can

11. Clouser, *Myth*, 1st ed, 217.
12. Ibid., 215.
13. Dooyeweerd, *New Critique,* I, 63.
14. Strauss, *Paradigms*, Preface.

be defended only by invoking a subjectivist priority assignment to sensory functioning and, thus, attributing to that functioning a status only God has.[15] Indirect frequentists presuppose a reductive metaphysics, whether or not they are aware of it.

It is helpful at this point to illustrate some practical implications of indirect frequentists' subjectivist mind-set, along with what can happen when they try to communicate with direct frequentists. I therefore review here a debate between the U.S. Fish and Wildlife Service's Division of Endangered Species, and some commentators external to the Service.[16] The debate concerned a then-recent study conducted to find whether the delta smelt should be listed as a threatened species, and to infer the causes of this fish's decline in prevalence. The record of the debate displays a collection of non-significant p-values (in the sense of exceeding the traditional threshold of *0.05* for statistical significance), and recounts that the Service determined

> ... threatened status for the delta smelt (*Hypomesus transpacificus*), pursuant to the Endangered Species Act of 1973, as amended (Act). This osmerid fish species occurs only in Suisun Bay and the Sacramento-San Joaquin estuary (known as the Delta) near San Francisco Bay, California. The delta smelt has declined nearly 90 percent over the last 20 years, and is primarily threatened by large freshwater exports from the Sacramento River and San Joaquin River diversions for agriculture and urban use.

The commentators, however, upon reviewing the study's statistical analyses,

---

15. Clouser, "General Relation."
16. US Fish and Wildlife Service, "Endangered and threatened."

> asserted that no listing determination could be made for the delta smelt because the Service has not demonstrated any statistically significant correlation between the factors suggested in the proposed rule as having contributed to the species' decline and its distribution and abundance.

Such a rejoinder reveals the direct frequentist stance that beliefs and decisions follow directly from statistical test results; statistical significance must lead to one kind of conclusion, and non-significance must lead to another kind.

The Service responded to the commentators as follows, reflecting the indirect frequentist attitudes that statistical significance is neither sufficient nor necessary for any particular conclusion, and that statistical test results are to be combined subjectively with non-statistical information:

> The Endangered Species Act requires the Service to base listing determinations upon the best available scientific and commercial data. The Service is not required to show statistical significance . . . and a lack of such statistical significance does not invalidate the analysis of the five factors upon which this listing determination is based. The complexity of the Delta ecosystem and the numerous stated factors contributing in time and space to the species' decline make it highly unlikely that any one factor would show a direct correlation with its distribution or abundance. . . . However, the precipitous decline in delta smelt abundance after 1981 coincides with a proportional increase in fresh water diversion by State and Federal water projects during the months when delta smelt are spawning (Moyle et al. 1992).

Most notable here is the Service's manner of argument: Despite a lack of statistical significance, the Service adjudged that sufficient evidence had been obtained to infer that the delta smelt was threatened by freshwater exports. This line of reasoning involves a decoupling of statistical inference from statistical testing results, so that those results serve as suggestive guides, not firm rules.

We should hardly be surprised if the commentators, in spite of the Service's response and likely under the influence of direct frequentism, continued to take exception to the Service's inference. When direct and indirect frequentist viewpoints collide, their non-negotiable commitments to mathematicism and subjectivism, respectively, are likely to prevent compromise or mutual understanding. The one paradigm sees optimal conclusions as products of mathematically processed empirical data; the other sees them as products of personal interpretation and intuition; and that is that. The PLI's analysis of the relations between overviews of reality and scientific theorizing, however, penetrates to the source of these inter-paradigmatic conflicts. It identifies the conflicts as reverberations of the conflicts between two overviews of reality—mathematicism and subjectivism.

7

The PLI and Subjective Bayesianism

Mathematicism, Subjectivism, and Subjective Bayesianism

THE PLI's overview of reality aims to be acceptable within the bounds set by Christian belief for such overviews. What statistical paradigms might, in turn, fit into the bounds this overview sets for scientific theories? At a minimum, such paradigms must steer clear of the mathematicism and subjectivism inherent in the three paradigms linked above with the nature and personality ideals.

Subjective bayesian analyses begin not with experimental data or mathematical principles, but with pre-analytic fiduciary beliefs. These beliefs are intertwined, at a multi-aspectual, "non-abstractive"[1] level, with theoretical insights concerning the biological, chemical, economic, and other types of functioning studied in the sciences in which statistics is applied. Subjective bayesian analyses next abstract, or focus on, the quantitative degrees of these beliefs, and express them in prior probability distributions. They then generate the likelihood functions of the param-

1. Runner, *Relation of the Bible*, 151.

eters using the observed data, and combine those functions with the priors, according to mathematical laws, to produce the parameters' posterior probability distributions. Finally, subjective bayesian analyses use these posteriors to derive the consequent final quantitative-fiduciary degrees of belief of hypotheses of interest.

Subjective bayesianism seems, therefore, not to entail the inter-aspectual reductions and disconnections posited by mathematicism or subjectivism. First, it makes no pretension that beliefs about scientific hypotheses can or must follow solely from quantitative data. It aims, rather, to combine those data with the degrees of pre-analytic beliefs people actually hold in the coherence of inter-aspectual meaning. Second, even though subjective bayesian analyses, like indirect frequentist ones, incorporate pre-analytic sensory functioning into its conclusions, they do not reduce the fiduciary aspect to the sensory aspect, as do indirect frequentist analyses. They rather combine that functioning with quantitative data according to mathematical rules. Their conclusions thus indicate what is proper, in a *normative* sense, to believe about hypotheses, given the prior and data. In other words, unlike indirect frequentism, subjective bayesianism relies on scientific "objects" to place fiduciary "limitations" on "the subject who does the knowing."[2]

Possible Objections to Subjective Bayesianism from the Perspective of the PLI

Statistical inference aims to provide fiduciary meaning about logical hypotheses, given quantitative data; surely, such a philosophically complex quest could be misdirected in a multitude of ways. Let us, therefore, be clear: To fit the PLI's constraints for scientific theories, a paradigm for statis-

2. Hart, *Understanding our World*, 232; Clouser, *Myth*, 1st ed, 214.

tical inference must do more than avoid the reductions committed by the other three paradigms considered here. More broadly, it must respect the boundaries between (at least) the fiduciary, logical, and quantitative aspects, as well as respect the subjection of beliefs to the laws of all the aspects.

Investigating fully whether subjective bayesianism fits these constraints is beyond my present scope; nonetheless, without taking up too much time or space here, I can mention here some potential conflicts between the PLI and this bayesianism, and briefly consider whether they are real or only apparent.

Does Forming Subjective Bayesian Priors Reduce Non-Quantitative Properties of Beliefs?

According to the PLI, functioning in each aspect in the list of aspects in Chapter 4 above presupposes functioning in all the aspects "earlier" in the list as well; functioning in each "earlier" aspect is a "precondition" for functioning in any "later" aspects. Thus, because beliefs function in the fiduciary aspect, which is the final aspect, we can expect them to exhibit properties of and obey the laws of the entire spectrum of aspects. Beliefs have *legal* properties, for instance; if someone believes her child is being physically attacked, she might be entitled or even obligated by law to impede the apparent attack, if possible. Beliefs possess an *ethical* dimension, too; for "love [an ethical function] believes all things."[3] Beliefs, by cohering with each other, can exhibit *aesthetic* harmony. A person's beliefs about the value of a manufactured product delimit what *economic* sacrifices he would make to obtain it.

We could, to be sure, continue to list properties of all the other aspects that are disclosed by beliefs, and laws from those aspects to which these beliefs are subject, as well. Our

3. 1 Cor 13:7, KJV.

ability to do so, however, alludes to a potential problem with both objective and subjective bayesianism: It seems to discredit these paradigms, by suggesting that forming priors reduces rich, multi-faceted beliefs to nothing but quantities, depreciating and obscuring non-quantitative properties of beliefs. Generating these priors would, then, be a reductive exercise.

Indeed, in an important sense, this apprehension concerning bayesianism is phrased too narrowly, for we might worry also about the end products of bayesian analyses—the posterior probabilities, estimates, and so forth that prescribe post-experimental degrees of beliefs. These post-experimental results seem to assume relations between quantitative and fiduciary properties and laws that are similar, at least, to those assumed by priors. Therefore, if priors could be reductive, then the same might be true for posteriors.

Concluding that constructing priors or posteriors is necessarily reductive would be premature, however, without first considering the PLI's analysis of abstraction, including how abstraction differs from reduction. In Chapter 5 above, I said a few words about the PLI's concept of "non-dissected," prescientific experience. I characterized that experience as the indispensable foundation of any scientific investigation. Scientific theorizing is "altogether different"[4] from prescientific experience. It proceeds in an analytic fashion—it separates something from concrete things. As scientists, we study things by concentrating on, or abstracting, the thing's properties of one or a few kind(s) from their wider context. We "pry apart reality into the diversity of aspects" and "pull something essential away from the structure of reality as it is given to naïve experience."[5] Indeed, it is precisely by examining the "perspective (aspect, way

4. Dooyeweerd, *Reformation and Scholasticism*, Chapter 3.
5. Ibid.

The PLI and Subjective Bayesianism 85

of being, mode, modality, function, facet) of reality"[6] from which things—including beliefs about scientific hypotheses—are investigated, that we differentiate each kind of science (such as biology, chemistry, and mathematics) from other kinds. Science is, then, not primary but secondary. It gives us an artificial dissection of reality.[7]

For example, a musical performance displays properties of many aspects: quantitative multiplicities of tones, spatial distances between musicians, kinetic movements of sound waves, and so forth. Even so, a linguist, as a particular type of scientist, might focus almost exclusively on the performance's symbolic properties, studying how the performance represents or accentuates certain features of other things. Concentrating on these properties conveys the advantage of gaining greater insights into them.[8] But we must never imagine that what is given, namely, the musical performance, is the same as those linguistic properties. "What is given can never be the artificial product of theoretical abstraction" and "[t]he modal aspect can never be the full reality we experience."[9] The scientific process of abstraction is not first, but second;[10] it cannot replace non-dissected prescientific experience, but must be used to augment and enhance that experience.

Abstraction does not entail reduction; on the contrary, it is a valid and necessary activity of science. So, if one established that forming subjective bayesian probability distributions is, or can be, abstraction instead of reduction, one would not only defuse an objection to subjective bayesianism, but also show that this statistical paradigm is

6. Strauss, *Paradigms*, 12.
7. Dooyeweerd, *Reformation and Scholasticism*, Chapter 3.
8. Clouser, *Myth*, 1st ed, 54; Rice, "What is a science?"
9. Dooyeweerd, *Reformation and Scholasticism*, Chapter 3.
10. Runner, *Relation of the Bible*, 125.

scientific in at least one respect. I will, then, illustrate a few abstractive features of forming these distributions.

As I mentioned, a musical performance can be investigated from various perspectives or aspects; the same can be said for beliefs in scientific hypotheses. A scientist of jurisprudence might investigate these beliefs from the standpoint of whether an accused followed his or her beliefs' legally binding ramifications. An economist might examine the effects of beliefs on a person's patterns of buying and selling. Statistical inference, on the other hand, seeks to identify how strongly one believes, or should believe, this or that hypothesis of interest. This inference focuses on—abstracts—beliefs' quantitative degrees and, therefore, investigates beliefs from a quantitative perspective. Let us consider how subjective bayesian inference, in particular, accomplishes this abstraction.

As noted in Chapter 3, subjective bayesians seek to form priors using whatever information is available about unknown statistical parameters. Two commonly implemented methods for gathering and synthesizing this information are elicitation and measurement of maximum betting odds. In elicitation, one or more people specify their degrees or extents of belief in relevant hypotheses. Usually, these people are specialists in the field in which statistical inference is being applied, and have the most thorough relevant knowledge available. A veteran engineer developing a prior for the average lifespan of a new electronic component, for instance, might draw on his or her past experiences with similar, more familiar electronic components, while taking into account the novel features of the new one. The interconnectedness the PLI identifies between the quantitative, fiduciary, physical, and logical aspects allows the engineer's partial knowledge concerning physical properties to manifest itself in degrees of beliefs.

Measurement of maximum betting odds, on the other hand, identifies a person's probabilities of hypotheses by asking questions like, "What is the most you would pay to enter into a wager in which you receive a dollar if hypothesis H is true, and nothing if H is false?" For instance, if H states that the average lifespan of the aforementioned component is less than 1,000 hours, and the engineer would pay up to 10 cents to enter into that wager, then his probability of H would be taken to be 10%. Here, the connections between the quantitative, fiduciary, physical, and economic aspects come to the fore, in that quantitative degrees of fiduciary beliefs concerning physical properties delimit the economic transactions in which the engineer would participate.

Thus, the elicitation method of forming subjective priors seeks to measure degrees of belief directly, whereas the betting odds method does so indirectly, in consort with economic properties. Either way, though, the statistician gradually narrows the scope of the investigation to the quantitative properties of fiduciary beliefs. Other properties of those beliefs fade into the background, where they remain while the inferential analyses are conducted. This focusing does not necessarily entail reduction, however, for it doesn't require one to assume that non-quantitative properties are caused by, less important than, the same as, or independent from quantitative ones. This suggests that reduction can be avoided while forming subjective bayesian prior probability distributions.

Most of what I have said concerning subjective bayesian priors carries over to subjective bayesian posteriors. Posteriors, like priors, are instruments for abstraction and concentrated study of the quantitative degrees of belief we might have in scientific hypotheses. As with priors, posteriors can be developed and used non-reductively as long as no claim is made that the degrees of beliefs they measure are more important or basic than, or independent from, those beliefs' other properties.

Dealing with posteriors non-reductively does, however, require something distinct from using priors non-reductively. This additional criterion stems from the uses—specifically, the practical decisions—to which posteriors may be put, after statistical analyses are complete. A government official, for example, might decide whether to permit a particular placement of an underground electricity transmission cable, based on (having studied the constellation of relevant factors) the posterior probability of the hypothesis H that a seismic shift will occur in the area and sever the cable. Plainly, the decision cannot rest on that probability alone; economic, social, moral, biological, and other types of properties and laws affect the decision as well. We must not assert, then, that permitting or forbidding the cable's placement is optimal economically, socially, morally, or biologically, simply because the post-experimental certainty of H [the posterior probability $Pr(H|x)$] exceeds or falls below some arbitrary threshold.

Are Subjective Bayesian Conclusions Subjectivist?

Priors influence final analytic conclusions; for example, a greater prior probability of any hypothesis H leads to stronger conclusions for H or, at least, weaker conclusions against it. One might allege, then, that subjective bayesianism, by using priors chosen by people, allows these people, rather than external, objective reality, to determine statistical conclusions. In that case, this paradigm would be as subjectivist as is indirect frequentism; the only practical difference would be that, whereas indirect frequentism begins with deductive, objective statistical analyses, only later to subjectively invent inductive meanings for their results, subjective bayesianism sets a subjectivist course for itself from the start, injecting subjectivity into its analyses themselves: "A major

The PLI and Subjective Bayesianism 89

difficulty [with bayesianism], of course, is deciding on the prior distribution. This is going to influence the conclusions of the study, yet it may be a subjective synthesis of the available information, so the same data analyzed by different investigators could lead to different conclusions."[11]

The indictment of subjective bayesian conclusions as hopelessly subjectivist depends, however, on the premises that subjective priors both

- are based on people's preferences, hopes, fears, and other personal idiosyncrasies, and
- markedly impact subjective bayesian conclusions.

These premises are false or at least overblown. The first is less true than it might seem because those constructing priors are to be aware of, and rely on, as much experience and knowledge as is available concerning the hypotheses being evaluated. According to the PLI, such awareness and reliance are possible because, according to the PLI, "[k]nowledge and understanding do not start with the subject as if knowledge has to bridge an original gulf between the two . . . To [speak of such a gulf], we have to ignore that in actual life we experience ourselves in coherence with the world around us. . . . [K]nowledge presupposes that we are in a relationship already."[12] Thus, we can usually expect two or more analysts having the same pre-analytic information about the same hypotheses, in most cases, to substantially agree on their priors; furthermore, upon request, they can cite reasons for the particular priors they might choose.

Despite those links from objective reality to knowing subjects to subjective priors, objective bayesians may rejoin that objective priors, being founded on sure principles (such as uniformity and non-informativity), are more trustwor-

11. Bland and Altman, "Bayesians and frequentists."
12. Geertsema, "Dooyeweerd's transcendental critique."

thy than subjective priors, because quantitative and logical properties and laws provide the most reliable, "objective" experience. Yet, if that were true, then all knowledge that cannot be understood in logical and mathematical terms should be disqualified from influencing scientific conclusions. Such reasoning regards the quantitative and logical aspects as more basic or real than other aspects and, therefore, as divine or semi-divine. A Christian overview of reality, in contrast, ascribes the same validity and reliability to every aspect. Thus, economic properties and laws, for instance, are no less objective or real than quantitative and logical ones.

The facts that "we experience ourselves in coherence with the world around us," and that all the aspects are equally created and real, do not, admittedly, guarantee the absolute accuracy of subjective priors. The PLI does not advance any "uncritical theory" that pretends "reality in itself" can "imprint a perfectly adequate picture upon . . . human consciousness."[13] Nor does it guarantee that such a picture, if so imprinted, would be completely accurately translated into a subjective prior. Whenever non-quantitative laws and properties are used to form a quantitative subjective prior, the connections between them and the prior are nonetheless somewhat loose and indirect. A scientist beginning to form a subjective prior probability *Pr(H)* of an economic hypothesis *H*, for instance, might think carefully about his incomplete understanding of other relevant economic laws and properties. Such understanding would include what he knows about the results of any previous experiments and studies that make *H* more or less plausible. The scientist might then adjudge his resulting sensory, affective strength of belief in *H* and, subsequently, his quantitative degree of belief in *H*. He would, ultimately, linguistically symbolize that degree of belief, with an expression such as "*Pr(H)=70%*," although he might not

---

13. Dooyeweerd, *Reformation and Scholasticism*, Chapter 3.

quibble with another researcher, armed with the same knowledge, who assesses that same *Pr(H)* as only, say, *60%*.

Forming subjective priors is, therefore, not completely precise or fail-safe. It involves several steps and, at each step, one's incomplete understanding of relevant properties and laws can be distorted, unintentionally or even intentionally. For example, the scientist might fail to distinguish beliefs about hypotheses from what is hoped or feared to be true about hypotheses. He also might mistake his own beliefs for the commonly accepted beliefs of his peer group, or of practitioners in his field of science in general. Any failure to differentiate between the intended set of beliefs and other, extraneous factors may, to some extent, distort the prior and cause it to mislead. Such distortions should be minimized, for they make subjective priors subjective in a negative sense.

The possibility of subjective priors distorting degrees of belief does not, however, make such priors hopelessly subjective or non-scientific, for several reasons. First, several kinds of steps can be taken to reduce the potential for unintentional distortions. One commonly used procedure towards that end is the system of eliciting each important degree of belief several different ways, or using several different phrasings of the same question, and ensuring the mutual consistency of the results. Second, concerns about intentional distortions can be alleviated by eliciting degrees of beliefs from subject matter experts who do not stand to benefit from whatever the analyses might conclude. Indeed, the practice of employing disinterested parties to make or at least oversee all types of key decisions of scientific investigations improves the credibility and trustworthiness of such investigations. Third, both unintentional and intentional distortions of a degree of belief can be avoided or lessened by eliciting the degree from each of several specialists, or from those specialists as a group.

The second premise above, that subjective priors markedly impact bayesian conclusions, is true only to the extent the evidence from the data is weak. Admittedly, the prior together with that evidence determines the conclusions. However, the "principle of stable estimation" shows that, "provided the sample is sufficiently large, no great precision is required when describing the prior distribution in order to arrive at a correct and relatively precise posterior distribution."[14] This stability arises because, as more data accumulate, their effects on conclusions rapidly eclipse the effects of priors. In fact, any differences between two or more analysts' posterior probabilities due to differences between priors vanish, even with moderate sample sizes.

In summary, the conclusions of a subjective bayesian analysis need not be subjectivist, for two main reasons: The relationships that exist pre-analytically between scientists and scientific subject matter supply a valid foundation for constructing priors, and any differences in conclusions resulting from differences in priors are usually inconsequential.

Can Likelihood Ratios Support an Objective System of Inference?

As observed in Chapter 3, evidentialism appears to offer a system of objectively measuring the evidence conveyed by a set of data for one hypothesis, H_1, vis-à-vis another, H_2. This raises two questions, at least: First, does this paradigm comprise a more objective system of statistical inference than subjective bayesianism? Second, does the possibility of quantifying statistical evidence based on the data alone refute the PLI's contention that science must be founded on prescientific experience?

Two features of evidentialism show that these questions must be answered in the negative. To begin with, the

14. Howson and Urbach, *Scientific Reasoning*, 362.

likelihood ratios (*LRs*) evidentialism offers as conclusions do not constitute inferences. Statistical inference, I have said, consists of assessing the credibility of statistical hypotheses. In contrast, any *LR* indicates merely the degree to which the observed data change the odds of one hypothesis versus another. More technically, the *LR* $f(x|H_1)/f(x|H_2)$, times the pre-experimental odds $Pr(H_1)/Pr(H_2)$ of H_1 versus H_2, yields the inferential post-experimental odds $Pr(H_1|x)/Pr(H_2|x)$ of H_1 versus H_2:

$$f(x|H_1)/f(x|H_2) \times [Pr(H_1)/Pr(H_2)] = Pr(H_1|x)/Pr(H_2|x).$$

A *LR* can change the odds of one hypothesis versus another, but not create such an odds based on the data alone. Therefore, the evidence from the data reflected in the *LR* can contribute to inference, but it cannot on its own amount to inference. Whatever inference that might be done making use of *LRs* requires a foundation of prescientific degrees of belief, no less than bayesianism does. These degrees, as symbolized in mathematical expressions for prior odds, may reflect subjective elements, in the senses identified in the "Are Subjective Bayesian Priors Subjectivist?" section above. Therefore, evidentialism cannot deliver a greater level of objectivity in statistical inference than subjective bayesianism does. Furthermore, the fact that evidentialism requires prior odds of hypotheses to make inferential statements actually affirms the PLI's claims about the necessity of the prescientific as a foundation for science.

Evidentialism incorporates subjectivity and affirms the prescientific as a necessary foundation for scientific investigation in another manner, as well: the way it handles composite hypotheses (rather than simple hypotheses). To explain this paradigm's treatment of composite hypotheses, I begin by considering its treatment of simple hypotheses. A simple hypothesis is one that specifies but a single value for each unknown statistical parameter. For instance, let us assume the datum $x=7$ was obtained from a normal distribution having variance 36. If H_1 states that the mean μ ("mu") of that distribution is exactly 5, then H_1 is a simple hypothesis. The PDF $f(x|H_1)$ of x assuming H_1 can, thus, be computed merely algebraically, as

$$f(x|H_1) = f(x|\mu=5)$$
$$= exp[-(7-5)^2/(2*36)]/\sqrt{(36*2\pi)} = 0.063.$$

Here, "$exp(p)$" is the exponential function, which raises the transcendental number e (approximately 2.72) to the power p. Similarly, if H_2 states that $\mu = 4$, then $f(x|H_2)=0.059$. The LR of H_1 versus H_2,

$$f(x|H_1) / f(x|H_2) = 0.063 / 0.059 = 1.072,$$

exceeds 1, showing that the datum favors H_1 more than H_2. Furthermore, multiplying the prior odds of H_1 versus H_2 by this LR supplies the posterior odds of H_1 versus H_2. Thus, a LR can fairly objectively gauge the evidence—conceived the evidentialist way—in x for one simple hypothesis relative to another although, admittedly, some subjectivity is involved in assuming that the datum $x=7$ was realized from a normal distribution.

Nonetheless, measuring evidence using LRs is not usually as easy as it was in the above situation, in that simple statistical hypotheses are useful in only a small minority of statistical applications. The parameters about which most hypotheses make statements are almost always on a continuum, and any single value for such a parameter has probability 0. Therefore, in most situations, to have any probability greater than 0, a hypothesis must be composite, meaning that it stipulates a composite range for the parameter, such as (a,b) where $a < b$.

For instance, an experiment might be conducted to study the average lifespan μ of a specific electrical component. Generally, a lifespan may conceivably be any non-negative number. Therefore, to possess any positive probability, any hypothesis H_1 about μ would have to stipulate a continuous range for μ, such as *0 < μ < 20*. The hypothesis that μ=*13*, say, would in most situations have probability zero.

The fact that, in most practical applications, the statistical hypotheses of interest are composite causes trouble for the evidentialist hoping to measure evidence without a prescientific foundation. When the H_1 or H_2 or both in the *LR* are composite, computing the PDFs corresponding to them requires pre-analytic deliberations analogous to those required in bayesianism. Suppose, for example, that H_1 is the composite hypothesis which states that μ is 5 or 6. The PDF *f(x|H_1)* must, then, be computed as a linear combination of *f(x|μ =5)* and *f(x|μ =6)*:

$$f(x|H_1) = \alpha f(x|\mu =5)+(1-\alpha)f(x|\mu =6),$$

for some α ("alpha") between 0 and 1. More than algebra is needed here, in that the value of α must be determined, presumably as the prior probability *Pr(μ=5|H_1)*. This example illustrates, then, the fact that evidentialism cannot evaluate evidence without incorporating the prescientific, except in the rare cases where both H_1 and H_2 are simple hypotheses. To sum up, we can conclude that not only are prior probabilities needed to make inferences about hypotheses; they are almost always needed even to evaluate the evidentialists' type of evidence.

8

A Paradigmatic Synthesis

I HAVE identified some constraints that Christian and humanist religious beliefs place on overviews of reality, and constraints that certain overviews of reality place on statistical theorizing. I have also put forward reasons for assessing subjective bayesianism, but not the other paradigms identified in this essay, as consistent with the PLI's Biblically-consistent constraints on statistics.

A possible misunderstanding needs to be avoided, however, regarding what the PLI's overview of reality finds objectionable within direct frequentism, indirect frequentism, and objective bayesianism. To head off that misunderstanding, we must distinguish between these paradigms themselves, and the mathematical results they usually employ. The paradigms, as mentioned in Chapter 3, are systems of theories concerning what may be concluded about statistical hypotheses, given statistical data. As the "ism" in each of their names suggests, the paradigms are doctrines or systems of principles. These results, on the other hand, are the quantitative ends of mathematical calculations, such as p-values, maximum likelihood estimates, confidence intervals, N-P hypothesis tests, objective bayesian posterior probabilities and so on. Each paradigm influences what calculations will be performed, and determines how the results of those calculations will be interpreted.

The distinction between statistical paradigms and statistical results already came up in the discussion, in Chapter 3, of maximum likelihood (ML) estimation. I observed, in that context, that maximum likelihood estimators (MLEs), as mathematical results, appear fairly innocuous, in that little seems wrong with merely performing numeric calculations. Direct frequentism as a paradigm, however, prescribes what inductive meanings may be gleaned from MLEs, and how these meanings may be gleaned. In particular, direct frequentism dictates that the researcher regard an MLE as the best estimate of the statistical parameter.

The mistake I wish to prevent concerning statistical paradigms and results is the misunderstanding that the results usually associated with one or more paradigms are reductive and, hence, conflict with the PLI's overview of reality. Rather, it is certain paradigms, and not the results, which are reductive, in their dogmatic, uncritical implementations of those results, including the situations in which the paradigms employ those results and the meanings the paradigms interpret the results to convey. Direct frequentism and objective bayesianism implement their results because they unjustifiably assume that valid fiduciary content about statistical hypotheses can be derived directly from mathematical calculations, reducing fiduciary meaning to quantitative meaning. Indirect frequentism, conversely, implements its results because it assumes that fiduciary content can be intuited subjectively in the mind from some mixture of those results together with other evidence and considerations. In the process, indirect frequentism reduces fiduciary meaning to feelings and preferences, fracturing the coherence between quantitative and fiduciary laws.

The reductive character of those three paradigms does not mean that all the results they typically implement are intrinsically reductive. In fact, in some circumstances, as I will now show, some of these results may be used non-reductively, and may even be helpful. However, I will not present a complete taxonomy of the circumstances in which these results may be used these ways.

I propose that the results commonly associated with frequentism and objective bayesianism be implemented in the framework of a particular synthesis between all four paradigms described in this essay. The main rationale of this synthesis is that, in various situations, some of these results can justifiably be reinterpreted as approximate subjective bayesian results, while requiring fewer calculations and less intensive measurement of subjective prior beliefs. In many applications, the possibility of such reinterpretations arises from the fact that, as stated in Chapter 3, frequentist as well as bayesian methods make use of the likelihood functions $Pr(x|H)$ and $f(x|H)$. Thus, these results can on occasion support non-reductive inferences that are (almost) as dependable as inferences that would be based on subjective bayesian calculations, while requiring less work.

To illustrate this synthesis, consider the following experimental situation. An ornithologist wants to investigate the average length μ ("mu") of the beaks of the adult female of a newly discovered bird species. He obtains a sample of 20 such birds, measures their beaks, and calculates the sample mean as *y=3.2* cm and sample variance as *s²=0.7*. This sample mean *y=3.2* is the maximum likelihood estimate (MLE) of μ, since *3.2* is the value of μ which maximizes the likelihood $f(y|μ)$. The standard error of this mean (s.e.m.) is the square root of *0.7/20,* or *0.187*. Almost any frequentist analyst would, therefore, report "*y=3.2, s.e.m.=0.187*" (possibly accompanied by a confidence interval, which is a simple function of the sample mean and variance) as the experimental result.

It is important to note that reporting a sample mean and s.e.m., with no interpretation of these results, is not statistical inference. Inference, I have said, consists of making fiduciary statements concerning hypotheses. Direct frequentist inference, for example, would go on to claim the sample mean, *y=3.2*, implies a direct inference about μ, specifically, that *3.2* is the most credible value of μ. This inference would, furthermore, interpret *0.187* as a measure of variation concerning μ around *y*.

One extremely simple reporting technique in this experiment would be merely calculating a sample mean and s.e.m. Deriving the subjective bayesian post-experimental distribution of probability for μ, though, requires a bit more work. First, it demands specifying the prior distribution of probability about μ. Let us assume that, pre-experimentally, the most probable value of μ was 5cm, but that any value for μ even remotely close to 5cm was possible (although, of course, average beak lengths less than 0cm are inconceivable). Hence, say that a subjective bayesian decided the pre-experimental probability distribution *g(*μ*)* for μ was approximately normal with a mean of 5 and a variance of 2.

This bayesian must not only specify exactly his prior beliefs; he must perform some calculations that are a little more involved than the direct frequentist's. Although here I pass over their details, these calculations show that the most probable value of μ is *3.231* and the level of uncertainty around that value is *0.185*. These values are almost indistinguishable from *y* and the s.e.m. Consequently, even though *y* and the s.e.m. are statements about the data, they approximate the subjective bayesian conclusions quite closely. What is more, they were easier to derive than the subjective bayesian's inferences, and they didn't require as much measurement of subjective prior beliefs. In this particular experiment, then, the additional effort required by a subjective bayesian analysis didn't lead to numeric results much different from *y* and the s.e.m.

Many writers have dealt with correspondences between results usually implemented by direct frequentism, indirect frequentism, and objective bayesianism on the one hand, and subjective bayesian results on the other. They have also discussed some circumstances necessary or sufficient for such correspondences. Casella and Berger[1] identified a range of conditions under which the one-sided p-value will be close to the posterior probability of a tested one-sided hypothesis. Additionally, as mentioned above, the stable estimation principle establishes conditions under which choices between prior distributions for statistical parameters don't markedly influence posterior distributions; these conditions can aid the analyst, in any particular situation, in deciding whether an objective bayesian analysis will yield conclusions approximately equal to what subjective bayesian methods would yield.[2] Schield even advised taking advantage of potential correspondences between bayesian and frequentist results in the classroom, by teaching students to make bayesian statements about degrees of belief using hypothesis test results.[3] Howard discussed the advantages and disadvantages of various approaches to explaining the relations between bayesian and frequentist reasoning using 2×2 contingency tables.[4]

All the same, we must not expect every frequentist analysis to correspond to a reasonable bayesian one. Berger and Sellke, for instance, examined differences between the p-value from a two-sided significance test and the corresponding bayesian posterior probability of the tested hypothesis, under what these authors deemed reasonable priors, including what might be called "uniform" priors for two-sided

---

1. Casella and Berger, "Reconciling bayesian and frequentist."
2. Howson and Urbach, *Scientific Reasoning*, 362.
3. Schield, "Using bayesian inference."
4. Howard, "The 2 by 2 table."

A Paradigmatic Synthesis 101

testing.[5] They showed that the p-value is smaller, and often much smaller, than the bayesian posterior probability.

I am not, therefore, identifying any new similarities between conclusions of different statistical paradigms. However, I do suggest that the PLI's analysis of the religious control of statistical theorizing adds something highly significant to the literature dealing with those similarities—it motivates the analyst to take advantage of the conveniences of some frequentist and objective bayesian techniques, while avoiding the reductions those paradigms entail.

Without going into meticulous detail, I propose that the goals of both convenience and non-reduction can be met by planning any inferential statistical analysis according to the following general stages. The statistician should first identify a set of various bayesian and frequentist techniques which can be expected to yield satisfactory answers (after reinterpretation, as needed) to the scientific questions at hand. Then, out of that set he or she should select a few frequentist or objective bayesian analyses, if any exist, which would be meaningfully simpler or faster to conduct than the best subjective bayesian analysis. The next step is to assess, at least roughly, the degree to which we can expect those frequentist or objective bayesian analyses to produce results approaching the results of the subjective bayesian analysis. Finally, the analyst can compare the various analytic options, in terms of such factors as ease of implementation, analytic resource use, clarity of interpretation and, perhaps most importantly, accuracy (including rough conformity, at least, to Bayes' Theorem and, therefore, to the definition of conditional probability). The losses associated with providing sub-optimal inferences are also important to consider, since greater potential losses will warrant achieving greater

---

5. Berger and Sellke, "Testing a point null."

accuracy, even if doing so requires larger expenditures of analytic resources.

Among the factors guiding choices of calculations and results, though, one factor stands out as non-negotiable—the researcher must remain attentive to the fact that the results usually associated with frequentism and objective bayesianism convey valid inductive meaning insofar as they approximate subjective bayesian results. Non-reductive statistical inference acknowledges the dependence of posterior beliefs on prior beliefs (so that prescientific experience is recognized as the foundation for statistical inference). It also carries normative meaning and, thus, respects the coherence between fiduciary and quantitative laws. Subjective bayesianism is one paradigm, and the only paradigm discussed here, which meets both of these criteria. Thus, without the goal in mind of approximating subjective bayesian inference, the researcher is apt to produce and interpret frequentist and objective bayesian results even when doing so ignores important prescientific information or breaks that inter-aspectual coherence. In short, one way and, perhaps, the best way to ensure frequentist and objective bayesian results are interpreted inductively only when conditions warrant such interpretations is to maintain full awareness of the two necessary links in justifying such interpretations—the grounding of statistical inference in prescientific experience and the coherence between the fiduciary and quantitative aspects.

Indeed, it is entirely possible to overestimate how often bayesian and frequentist results will coincide. I was first alerted to the prevalence of such mistaken expectations while attending a presentation by a world-renowned authority on frequentist group-sequential significance testing methods. Someone in the audience brought up the merits of bayesian approaches to sequential analysis. The speaker tried to quell discussion about these merits by calling the bayesian-frequentist controversies a red herring. In particular, he claimed that the differences between bayesian and frequentist inferences were not important, since these "two approaches" yield the "same answers" as long as a uniform bayesian prior is used. Out of the 100 or so professional statisticians in the room, some with decades of statistical experience, I was the only one to protest against that assertion. At this point in the present book, it should be obvious that such a claim is erroneous from a number of angles:

- Bayesianism is not a single "approach," but rather at least two. Even in the situations in which both objective and subjective bayesianism would implement uniform priors, they would do so for very different reasons.
- The quantitative differences between the results usually produced by bayesian and frequentist analyses can be marked and extremely important, even when using uniform priors.
- Even when bayesian and frequentist results do coincide quantitatively, frequentist "answers" are frequencies of data, whereas bayesian answers are certainties regarding hypotheses.

To illustrate briefly the consequences of indiscriminately drawing inferences from results usually associated with frequentism and objective bayesianism, let us reflect on what could happen if, before measuring the 20 bird beaks in the experiment above, the ornithologist had additional information about μ. Let's say he had studied the bird's diet and concluded that beak lengths between 3cm and 7cm would best equip the bird for gathering and consuming food. While this knowledge might not affect the pre-experimentally most probable value for μ, it would probably reduce the variation in probability concerning μ from *2* to, say, *0.7*. This additional information would change the *a posteriori* most probable value of μ to *3.286*, which exceeds the previous most probable value and, hence, differs more from the MLE of *3.2*. So, the smaller prior spread of probability regarding µ causes the *a posteriori* most credible value to diverge further from the value of *y=3.2* the direct frequentist would conclude is most credible. Whether the greater difference from *3.2* is sufficient to disqualify the direct frequentist interpretation of *y* depends on how great are the consequences of sub-optimal statistical inference.

A researcher might, then, interpret results typically associated with frequentism and objective bayesianism inductively when such interpretations are erroneous or, at least, not justified. The possibility of such a mistake is not, however, the only reason that researchers implementing the type of synthesis I am proposing here must remain fully aware of these distinctions between paradigms. Another reason is pedagogic: Schield,[6] Banatero,[7] and others assert that teaching students to interpret frequentist test results only as statements about data, rather than statements about hypotheses, is difficult at best. Some of these writers claim further that only when bayesian reasoning is explained, along with its differences from frequentist reasoning, do large numbers of learners pick up on the purely deductive meanings of frequentist statements. These writers conclude that teaching bayesian reasoning is a crucial step in teaching the mathematically justified implications of frequentist results and enabling students to avoid misinterpreting these results.

The principal reason, however, for remaining conscious of the fact that objective bayesian posterior probability distributions, p-values, confidence intervals, hypothesis test results and so on convey valid inductive meaning only inasmuch as they come adequately close to subjective bayesian results is this: From a Christian perspective, the motiva-

6. Schield, "Using bayesian inference."
7. Banatero, "Controversies," 80–84.

tion for anything spoken or done matters as much as do the words and deeds themselves.

Abraham Booth (1734–1806), an English pastor, made this point in the course of urging Christians to perform everything with the end in mind of glorifying God and serving Him, rather than earning salvation or avoiding condemnation: "To constitute a work truly good, it must be done from a right principle, performed by a right rule, and intended for a right end."[8] From a Biblical point of view, a deed, even if outwardly noble and helpful, could nonetheless be carried out for wrong reasons. Such a deed is neither proper nor pleasing to God.

A person may give alms, for instance, for the proper reason of showing gratitude for the forgiveness of sins Christ has accomplished on the Cross, or for the improper reason of trying to obligate God to increase the person's reward—or to decrease his punishment. He may also give alms with the expectation of receiving something in return from those receiving the alms. Even if the external effect of giving alms is the same in all these cases, the action signifies nothing if not grounded in love, that is, in a will to obey God and in a selfless concern for the welfare of others.[9]

Statistical analyses must, then, be done for the right reasons, and not merely arrive at "right conclusions." This means that, even if a reductive analysis leads to the same inferences as would a non-reductive one, its reductions nonetheless prevent it from maintaining consistency with the PLI. An indirect frequentist's inferences, for example, could concur with the prescriptive (for degrees of belief) conclusions of a subjective bayesian analysis. Despite this concurrence, his conclusions remain reductive and inconsistent with the PLI, in that they are obtained from his in-

8. Booth, *Reign of Grace,* 201.
9. I Cor 13:1–3; see also I Chron 28:9 and I Cor 4:5.

ner dispositions, states of mind, preferences, and so forth, rather than from a voluntary submission to the implications of quantitative observations—along with the quantitative properties and laws with which God upholds the world—for fiduciary beliefs.

To summarize this chapter, I have contended that the p-values, hypothesis test results, objective bayesian posterior probability distributions, and other results usually associated with direct frequentism, indirect frequentism, and objective bayesianism can be implemented non-reductively, even though these paradigms themselves are reductive. Specifically, in some circumstances, these statistical results approximate subjective bayesian conclusions. When they do so, conclusions can be drawn from them that respect the bounds the PLI's overview of reality sets for statistical theorizing.

9

Conclusions

THE INCONSISTENCIES between the PLI's overview of reality and three of the statistical paradigms discussed in this book—direct frequentism, indirect frequentism, and objective bayesianism—do not, then, render all the results routinely derived by these paradigms powerless to aid researchers. At the same time, the apparent coherence between that overview of reality and subjective bayesianism does not imply that the PLI necessarily endorses every subjective bayesian analysis. Any statistical analysis, being a human activity, is subject to omissions of relevant information, mistakes in calculations, misinterpretations, and other types of errors. No statistical paradigm can save us from or prevent all human dishonesty or error. Moreover, forming subjective bayesian priors does, admittedly, afford opportunities for accidental or deliberate misrepresentation of extra-experimental information.

A subjective bayesian translating his or her prior beliefs into a prior who has a strong interest in the analysis justifying one conclusion or another could, perhaps even subconsciously, over- or under-represent his or her certainties, swaying the analysis towards his or her favor (even if, as pointed out in the "Are Subjective Bayesian Priors Subjectivist?" section above, the effects of choices of priors do usually wane as more data accumulate). This sort of bias can be considered a failure to separate beliefs from preferences, and would undoubtedly be detrimental. In all these ways, subjective bayesian analysis is by no means foolproof and is not guaranteed to lead automatically to truth; it requires analysts to exercise honesty and care, and requires those who put analytic conclusions to use to trust the analysts. Nor have I spoken here of all the objections raised against subjective bayesianism or, indeed, bayesianism in general, or claimed that the PLI could be used to defend this paradigm against all of them.

Nonetheless, it is not clear that these objections, along with the possibility of errors or misrepresentations in subjective bayesian analyses, invalidate these analyses. Nor do they show the other paradigms identified in this essay to be as helpful or accurate as subjective bayesianism. Objective bayesians and direct frequentists generate statistical inferences solely from empirical data and logical and mathematical principles, claiming that science must separate itself from purportedly "unscientific" opinions, expert knowledge, and impressions.[1] Indirect frequentists, conversely, try to merge abstract statistical test results with prior opinions and knowledge according to sensory feelings, intuition and states of mind. Objective bayesians have not shown that abstract mathematical principles for priors can adequately reflect or prescribe pre-analytic beliefs about unknown statistical quantities. Both direct and indirect frequentism, on the other hand, have ignored the "elephant in the room"—the basic difficulty that their statistical results (frequencies of data) are deductive statements, rather than the inductive statements that would constitute inference.

One implication of the deductive character of frequentist results, as opposed to the inductive character of bayesian

---

1. As with Fisher, for instance, who "wanted to both reject the Bayesian cake and eat it, too" (Gigerenzer, "Superego, ego," 315).

ones, is that drawing inferences from the former involves as much, if not more, assumption-making as does drawing inferences from the latter. As pointed out in Chapter 3, many researchers worry that subjective bayesian priors inject unacceptable degrees of subjectivity into statistical inference. These researchers don't seem to fully appreciate that drawing inferences from frequentist results requires assumptions of a more fundamental sort—assumptions concerning the meanings that frequencies of data convey about hypotheses. Direct frequentism assumes these frequencies can be reinterpreted as direct statements about the plausibility of hypotheses; indirect frequentism regards these frequencies as evidence (albeit undefined or vaguely defined) about hypotheses. These assumptions have no mathematical or logical justification. We cannot, therefore, agree with allegations, such as those cited in Chapter 3, that bayesianism requires more assumptions, or involves more subjectivity, than frequentism does.

The persistent attempts to defend direct and indirect frequentism and objective bayesianism in the face of these and other oft-cited objections, epitomize well the "bizarre, implausible lengths to which modern reduction theories have been driven in trying to show that the most diverse types of things actually have the same basic nature."[2] Yet, the effects identified by the PLI of religious beliefs on overviews of reality and, thereby, on scientific theorizing, account for this stubbornness. In particular, humanism's science and personality ideals, through their elevations of the quantitative, logical, and sensory aspects, each delimit a range of acceptable answers to the central question of statistical inference described above. These statistical paradigms have simply selected their divergent answers to that question from those ranges.

2. Clouser, *Myth*, 1st ed, 203.

Subjective bayesianism, unlike direct frequentism and objective bayesianism, incorporates pre-analytic fiduciary beliefs as a legitimate and even necessary foundation for statistical inference. It calls on the scientist to consider all information relevant to hypotheses of interest, as he or she assesses degrees of belief in those hypotheses. It also fits well into the PLI's conception of science as an abstractive activity, in its handling of both prior and posterior probabilities. Furthermore, unlike indirect frequentism, subjective bayesianism respects the coherence between the fiduciary and quantitative aspects, the coherence that implies that beliefs exhibit not only fiduciary and sensory properties, but also quantitative properties, which must obey quantitative laws.

In light of these features of subjective bayesianism and the ways humanistic beliefs control theorizing, the relative unpopularity of this statistical paradigm is hardly surprising: Humanism's nature ideal will not acknowledge pre-analytic beliefs as a foundation for statistical inference, and humanism's personality ideal will not concede the coherence between the quantitative and fiduciary aspects and the equal ontological status of these aspects.

This essay, then, has demonstrated an important manner in which religious beliefs control statistical inference—they set bounds for overviews of reality which, in turn, set bounds for statistical paradigms. It has also identified some non-reductive features of subjective bayesianism, features that fit the bounds the PLI's overview of reality sets for scientific theories. I am not insinuating, however, that subjective bayesianism can solve all the philosophical problems of statistics, or automatically make an analysis "Christian." Furthermore, despite our best intentions, any attempt to develop Christian principles for statistics may suffer from pre-theoretical accommodations to non-Christian thought patterns.

For these reasons, and also because of the brevity of this essay, additional investigation is needed on many of the

Conclusions

topics laid out here. More thought must be given to the implications for statistics of the relations (irreducibility and coherence) between the fiduciary, logical, quantitative, and other aspects; that is to say, what else do these relations indicate concerning the fiduciary conclusions scientists can seek about logical hypotheses given quantitative data? Another area which merits attention relates to the biological, physical, economic, and other types of knowledge specific to the sciences in which statistics is applied: How do these types of knowledge influence fiduciary degrees of belief? These and other matters are worthy of careful consideration, as Christians who are statisticians prayerfully strive to "make every [statistical] thought obedient to Christ."[3]

---

3. 2 Cor 10:5.

Glossary

abstraction, scientific. The extraction or removal of an aspect (defined next) from a wider, multi-aspectual context, for the purpose of focusing on that aspect.[1]

aspect. A kind of property and law.[2]

aspect, fiduciary. The kind of property and law referring to or dealing with the "varying levels of reliability or trustworthiness a thing or person may have."[3]

belief, religious. A "belief in something as divine *per se* no matter how that is further described, where 'divine *per se*' means having unconditional non-dependent reality."[4]

deduction, scientific. Reasoning or making statements about the specific or known, having made assumptions concerning the general or unknown.

divine. That which is self-sufficient or self-existent. In other words, the divine is unconditionally, non-dependently real.[5]

error of the mean, standard. Maximum likelihood estimator of the standard deviation of the sample mean, given the population mean.

---

1. Clouser, *Myth*, 2nd ed, 64.
2. Ibid., 67.
3. Ibid., 246.
4. Ibid., 23.
5. Ibid., 19.

estimator, maximum likelihood. The value of the statistical parameter that maximizes the likelihood.

evidentialism. A statistical paradigm asserting that the purpose of statistical analysis is to investigate the evidence for one hypothesis H_1 vis-à-vis another H_2, as measured by the likelihood ratio $f(x|H_1)/f(x|H_2)$.[6]

exp(y). The mathematical exponential function e^y of y, for any real number y, where e is the transcendental number $e=2.718282\ldots$

frequency, relative. The proportion of times an event occurs in a series of trials or experiments.

function, probability density. A mathematical function f such that a) the probability that an unknown quantity lies between two points a and b is the integral of f from a to b, b) f is non-negative for all real numbers, and c) the integral of f over all real numbers is 1.

function, probability mass. A mathematical function f such that a) the probability that an unknown quantity equals a specific value x is $f(x)$, b) f is non-negative for all real numbers, and c) the sum of $f(x)$ over all real numbers x is 1.

humanism. A religious belief system asserting that humans, or some aspects thereof, are divine.

hypothesis, composite. A proposition that a statistical parameter is any one of a collection of values.

hypothesis, simple. A proposition that a statistical parameter is a specified value.

hypothesis, statistical. A proposition concerning a statistical parameter.

Ideal, Nature. The system of humanist religious beliefs that envisions humans establishing and demonstrating their understanding, control and domination

---

6. Royall, "On the probability," 774.

over the natural world, through the application of scientific methods. Also called Science Ideal.

Ideal, Personality. The system of humanist religious beliefs that envisions humans exercising complete autonomy in self-expression and feeling. Also called Freedom Ideal.

induction, scientific. Reasoning or making statements about the general or unknown, having observed the specific.

inference, statistical. Reasoning or making statements about statistical hypotheses, having collected quantitative data.

interval, confidence. A range of values, selected from a set of such ranges a specified proportion of which will, over many repetitions of an experiment, contain a statistical parameter of interest. Assume, for instance, that a particular experiment is run a million times and, after each experiment, a 95% confidence interval (CI) for a mean is calculated. Then, approximately 95% of those CIs will contain the mean.

level, statistical significance. In RA Fisher's earlier thinking, a conventional threshold of *0.05*, to be used with the p-value in deciding whether to ignore an experimental finding. In Fisher's later thinking, the *p* value of a significance test.[7] Alternatively, in a hypothesis test, a pre-selected probability of erroneously rejecting the tested hypothesis *H* when *H* is true.

likelihood. If X is a discrete variable, then the likelihood, or likelihood function, $f_X(x|H)$ of the hypothesis H is the probability X will take the value x, assuming H. If X is continuous, then for any numbers *a* and *b*, the integral from *a* to *b* of $f_X(x|H)dx$ is the probability

---

7. Gigerenzer, "Mindless Statistics," 592–93.

X will take a value between a and b, assuming H. Usually, the notation $f_X(x|H)$ is shortened to $f(x|H)$.

mean. The arithmetic average of a set of numbers. To calculate the mean of a countable set of numbers, add the numbers together and then divide the sum by the number of numbers. To calculate the mean of a continuous range of numbers, integrate $xf(x)dx$ over the range, where $f(x)$ is the probability density function of the numbers, and divide that integral by the integral of $f(x)dx$ over the same range.

N-P. Jerzy Neyman and Egon Pearson, the originators of statistical hypothesis testing.

p-value. The probability, in a hypothetical repetition of the experiment that was actually performed, of observing results at least as undermining to the tested hypothesis H as were those observed, assuming H. Commonly referred to as simply "p," the p-value is read a variety of ways, two common ones being as a measure of evidence against H and as the post-experimental probability of H.

paradigm, statistical. A system of theories concerning how to obtain or determine the degrees to which statistical hypotheses are credible or plausible, given empirical observations.

parameter, statistical. An unknown quantity that determines or describes, possibly along with other such parameters, the probability distribution of observable data.

posterior. The post-analytic probability distribution of a statistical parameter. Also called Posterior Distribution.

prescientific knowledge. Non-statistical, multi-aspectual, non-dissected knowledge.

Pr(A|B). The probability of Event A conditional on, or "given," Event B.

prior. The pre-analytic probability distribution of a statistical parameter. Also called Prior Distribution.

reduction. A priority assignment between two or more aspects of reality. One or more aspect(s) are reduced to one or more other(s), thereby according the reducing aspects a divinity status.[8] The reduced aspects are seen as the same as, or caused by, the reducing aspects, and thus less important or real than the reducing ones.

syllogism. A deductive argument having two premises and a conclusion.

test, hypothesis. As introduced by N-P, a (statistical) hypothesis test is a rule for directing a researcher's behavior in relation to two pre-specified statistical hypotheses, the "null hypothesis" H_0 and the "alternative hypothesis" H_1. If the observed test statistic T falls into the so-called "critical region" C, the researcher is to "reject" H_0 and "accept" H_1. The researcher is then to behave as if H_1 is true. If T falls outside of C, the researcher is to accept H_0 and behave as if H_0 is true. N-P forbade attaching epistemic meanings to hypothesis test results; however, for many years, scientists have customarily attached such meanings to these results.

test, significance. The statistical procedure that produces a p-value p. A single statistical hypothesis H is proposed, the data are collected, and then the test statistic and p are calculated.

transposition of conditioning. Explicitly or implicitly assuming that the probability of Event A given Event B is exactly or approximately equal to the probability of B given A.

---

8. Clouser, *Myth*, 2nd ed, 127.

variable, continuous. An observable quantitative outcome of an experiment or other data-gathering activity, that could take on any one value within an interval. For example, the height of a building is a continuous variable; it could take any non-negative value.

variable, discrete. An observable quantitative outcome of an experiment or other data-gathering activity, that could take on any one of a countable list of distinct values. For example, the number of buildings within a given geographic area is a discrete variable.

variance, sample. The mean squared error, from a sample mean, of the members of a sample. That is, if y is the sample mean of n observations x_1, x_2, ... x_n, the sample variance is the sum of the terms $(x_i - y)^2/n$ for $i = 1, 2, \ldots n$.

Bibliography

American Statistical Association. "What is statistics? What do statisticians do?" No pages. Accessed 10 June 2007. Online: http://www.amstat.org/careers/index.cmf?fuseaction=whatisstatistics.

Anderson, Robert. *Practical Statistics for Analytical Chemists.* 1st ed. New York: Van Nostrand Reinhold, 1987.

Barnes, David. "General acceptance versus scientific soundness: Mad scientists in the courtroom." *Florida State University Law Review 31*: 2 (2004) 303–33. Accessed July 6, 2007. Online: http://www.law.fsu.edu/journals/lawreview/downloads/312/barnes.pdf.

Batanero, Carmen. "Controversies around the role of statistical tests in experimental research," *Mathematical Thinking and Learning 2* (2003) 75–98.

Basden, A. *Christian Philosophy and Information Systems,* Salford, UK: Information Systems Institute, University of Salford, 2001. No pages. Accessed June 8, 2007. Online: http://www.dooy.salford.ac.uk/papers/cpis.html.

Bayes, Thomas. "An essay towards solving a problem in the doctrine of chances," *Philos Trans R Soc Lon 53* (1763) 370–418.

Berger, James. *Statistical Decision Theory and Bayesian Analysis.* 2nd ed. New York: Springer, 1985.

———. "Bayesian analysis: A look at today and thoughts of tomorrow." No pages. Prepared as a vignette for *Journal of the American Statistical Association.* Accessed Feb 16, 2004. Online: http://www.isds.duke.edu/~berger/papers/99-30.html.

Berger, J. and Berry, Donald. "Statistical analysis and the illusion of objectivity." *American Scientist 76* (1988), 159–65.

Berger, J. and Sellke, Thomas. "Testing a Point Null Hypothesis: The irreconcilability of P–values and evidence." *Journal of the American Statistical Association 82* (1987) 112–39.

Bland, J. and Altman, Douglas. "Bayesians and frequentists." *British Medical Journal 317* (1998) 1151–60.

Booth, Abraham. *The Reign of Grace*. 1976 ed. Swengel, Pennsylvania: Reiner Publications.

Brouwer, William. "Christian commitment and scientific theories." Toronto: Association for the Advancement of Christian Scholarship, no date.

Burdette, W. and Edmund Gehan. *Planning and Analysis of Clinical Studies*. Springfield, IL: Charles C. Thomas, 1970.

Calvin, John. *Institutes of the Christian Religion*. Philadelphia: Presbyterian Board of Publication and Sabbath–Day Work, 1902.

Casella, G. and Roger L Berger. "Reconciling bayesian and frequentist evidence in the one–sided testing problem," *Journal of the American Statistical Association 82* (1987) 106–11.

Chan, Hei and Darwiche, Adnan. "On the revision of probabilistic beliefs using uncertain evidence." *Artificial Intelligence. 163* (2005) 1, 67–90. Accessed July 27, 2007. Online: http://repositories.cdlib.org/postprints/622.

Chase, G. and Calvin Jongsma. "Bibliography of Christianity and Mathematics: 1910–1983." Accessed June 8, 2007. Online: http://www.messiah.edu/departments/mathsci/acms/bibliog.htm.

Chinn, S. "Statistics for the European Respiratory Journal." *European Respiratory Journal 18* (2001) 393–401.

Clouser, Roy. "Genesis on the origins of the human race." *Perspectives on Science and Christian Faith* 43 (1991): 2–13.

———. "On the general relation of religion, metaphysics and science." In *Facets of Faith and Science, Volume 2: The Role of Beliefs in Mathematics and the Natural Sciences*, edited by J.M. van der Meer, ch 3. Lanham: The Pascal Centre for Advanced Studies in Faith and Science/University Press of America, 1996.

———. "Replies to the comments of Le Morvan, Halvorson, and Ratzsh on 'Prospects for Theistic Science.'" *Perspectives on Science and Christian Faith* 58: 1 (2006) 23–27.

———. *The Myth of Religious Neutrality*. 1st ed. Notre Dame: Notre Dame Press, 1991.

———. *The Myth of Religious Neutrality*. 2d ed. Notre Dame: Notre Dame Press, 2005.

Cohen, Jacob. "Things I have learned (so far)." *Journal of the American Psychological Association 45*: 12 (1990) 1304–12.

D'Agostini, Giulio. "Confidence Limits: What is the problem? Is there the solution?" No pages. Contribution to the Workshop on Confidence Limits, CERN, Geneva, 17–18 January 2000. Accessed June 3, 2005. Online: http://www–zeus.roma1.infn.it/~agostini/clw.pdf.

Davidoff, Frank. "Standing statistics right side up." *Annals of Internal Medicine 130* (1999) 1019–21.

DeGroot, Morris. "Doing what comes naturally: Interpreting a tail area as a posterior probability or likelihood ratio." *Journal of the American Statistical Association 68:* 344 (1973) 966–69.

Diamond, G. and James Forrester. "Clinical trials and statistical verdicts: probable grounds for appeal." *Annals of Internal Medicine 98* (1983) 385–94.

Diamond, G. and Sanjay Kaul. "Prior convictions: Bayesian approaches to the analysis and interpretation of clinical megatrials." *Journal of the American College of Cardiology 43*: 11 (2004) 1929–39.

Dooyeweerd, Herman. *Roots of Western Culture*. Toronto: Wedge, 1979.

———. *Reformation and Scholasticism in Philosophy: Volume 2*. Lewiston, New York: Edwin Mellen Press, 1998.

———. *A New Critique of Theoretical Thought*. Translated by DH Freeman and H DeJongste. Philadelphia: Presbyterian and Reformed Publishing Company, 1984.

Edwards, AWF. *Likelihood*. Cambridge, UK: Cambridge University Press, 1972.

Efron, Bradley. "RA Fisher in the 21st Century." *Statistical Science 13*: 2 (1998) 95–122.

———. "Modern science and the bayesian–frequentist controversy." Accessed May 31, 2007. Online: http://www–stat.stanford.edu/~brad/papers/NEW–ModSci_2005.pdf.

Ellison, Aaron (2004). "Statistics and science, objectivity and truth." In *The Nature of Scientific Evidence,* edited by M. L. Taper and S. R. Lele. 362–7. Chicago: University of Chicago Press.

Fisher, Ronald. *Statistical Methods for Research Workers*. 1st ed. Edinburgh: Oliver and Boyd, 1925.

———. *Statistical Methods for Research Workers*. 9th ed. Edinburgh: Oliver and Boyd, 1944.

———. *The Design of Experiments*. 5th ed. Edinburgh: Oliver and Boyd, 1951.

———. "Statistical methods and scientific induction." *Journal of the Royal Statistical Society (B)*: 17 (1955) 69–77.

———. *Statistical Methods and Scientific Inference*. New York: Hafner, 1956.

Gay, Peter. *The Enlightenment: An Interpretation*. New York: Alfred A Knopf, 1967.

Geertsema, Henk. "Dooyeweerd's transcendental critique: transforming it hermeneutically." In *Contemporary Reflections on the Philosophy of Herman Dooyeweerd,* edited by Strauss, DFM and Michelle Botting. New York: Edwin Mellen Press, 2000.

Geertsema, Jan. "A Christian view of the foundations of statistics." *Perspectives on Science and Christian Faith 39* (1987) 158–64.

Gigerenzer, Gerd. "The superego, the ego, and the id in statistical reasoning." In *A Handbook for data analysis in the behavioral sciences: Methodological Issues,* edited by G. Keren and C. Lewis, 311–39. Hillsdale, NJ: Erlbaum, 1993.

———. "Mindless Statistics." *Journal of Socio–economics 33* (2004) 587–606.

Good, Irving. "The interface between statistics and philosophy of science." *Statistical Science 3:*4 (1988) 386–97.

Goodman, Steven. "Meta–analysis and evidence." *Controlled Clinical Trials 10* (1989) 188–204.

———. "p values, hypothesis tests and likelihood: Implications for epidemiology of a neglected historical debate." *American Journal of Epidemiology 137:*5 (1993) 485–95.

———. "Toward evidence–based medical statistics. 1: The p–value fallacy." *Annals of Internal Medicine 130* (1999) 995–1004.

———. "Toward evidence–based medical statistics. 2: The bayes factor." *Annals of Internal Medicine 130* (1999) 1005–13.

Goudzwaard, Bob. *Capitalism and Progress: A Diagnosis of Western Society* Toronto: Association for the Advancement of Christian Scholarship, 1979.

Guilford, J. P. *Fundamental Statistics in Psychology and Education.* 1st ed. New York: McGraw–Hill.

Hacking, Ian. *Logic of Statistical Inference.* New York: Cambridge University Press, 1965.

Haller, H. and Krauss, Stephan. "Misinterpretations of significance: A problem students share with their teachers?" *Methods of Psychological Research 7*, 1 (2002) 1–20.

Hart, Hendrik. *Understanding our World: An Integral Ontology.* Lanham, MD: University Press of America, 1984.

Hartley, Andrew. "The philosophy of the law idea and the role of the prescientific in statistical inference." *Journal of the Association of Christians in the Mathematical Sciences 1* (2004). Accessed June 20, 2007. Online: http://www.acmsonline.org/Hartley–04.pdf.

Hogg, R. and Allen Craig. *Introduction to Mathematical Statistics.* 4th ed. New York: Macmillan, 1978.

Hogg, R. and Elliot Tanis. *Probability and Statistical Inference*. 4th ed. New York: Macmillan, 1993.

Holzinger, Karl. *Statistical Methods for Students in Education*. Boston: Ginn and Company, 1928.

Howard, J.V. "The 2 by 2 Table: A discussion from a bayesian viewpoint," *Statistical Science 13*: 4 (1998) 351–67.

Howson, C. and Peter Urbach. *Scientific Reasoning: The Bayesian Approach*. Chicago: Open Court, 1993.

Hubbard, Raymond and Armstrong, J. Scott. "Why we don't really know what 'statistical significance' means: A major educational failure." *Journal of Marketing Education 28*: 2 (2006) 114–120.

Huntsberger, David. *Elements of Statistical Inference*. Boston: Allyn and Bacon, 1961.

Institute for Clinical Harmonization. *ICH Guideline E9: Statistical Principles for Clinical Trials*. 1998. Accessed June 5, 2007. Online: http://chinagmp.net/ICH/ich–files/E9.PDF.

Journal of Thoracic and Cardiovascular Surgery. "Statistical methods." *Journal of Thoracic and Cardiovascular Surgery 120* (2000) 1. Accessed July 6, 2007. Online: http://www.ctsnet.org/journals/jtcsstatisticalmethods.pdf.

Kalsbeek, L. "Introduction." In *Contours of a Christian Philosophy*, edited by Bernard and Josina Zylstra. Toronto: Wedge Publishing Foundation, 1975.

Kempthorne, Oscar. "Of what use are tests of significance and tests of hypotheses?" *Communications in Statistics–Theory and Methods A5*: 8 (1976) 763–77.

Kinnear, Thomas and Taylor, James. *Marketing Research: An Applied Approach*. 4th ed. New York: McGraw–Hill, 1991.

Kocher, Mininder and Zurakowski, David. "Clinical epidemiology and biostatistics: A primer for orthopaedic surgeons part 1." No pages. Accessed July 6, 2007. Online: http://www.orthojournalhms.org/volume5/manuscripts/ms06.htm.

Krams, Michael, et al. "The past is future: Innovative designs in acute stroke therapy trials," *Stroke 36* (2005) 1341. Accessed May 31, 2007. Online: http://stroke.ahajournals.org/cgi/content/full/36/6/1341.

Kuyper College. "About Kuyper." No pages. Accessed June 20, 2007. Online: http://www.kuyper.edu/About/AbrahamKuyper.aspx.

Lee, Elisa. *Statistical Methods for Survival Data Analysis*. 2d ed. New York: Wiley, 1992.

Lehmann, E.L. *Theory of Point Estimation*. New York: Wiley, 1983.

Bibliography

Mach, Ernst. In *Encyclopædia Britannica*. Retrieved June 4, 2007, from Encyclopædia Britannica Online: http://www.britannica.com/eb/article-9049725.

Maksoudian, Y Leon. *Probability and Statistics with Applications*. Scranton, Pennsylvania: International Textbook Company, 1969.

McClave, J. and Frank Dietrich. *Statistics*. 2d ed. San Francisco: Dellen Publishing, 1982.

McDaniel, C and Gates, R. *Marketing research: The impact of the internet*. 5th ed. Cincinnati, OH: South–Western, 2002.

McLean, Alan. "On the nature and role of hypothesis tests." Working Paper 4/2001. Australia: Monash University, Department of Econometrics and Business Statistics.

Mendenhall, William, et al. *Mathematical Statistics with Applications*. 3d ed. Boston: Duxbury, 1986.

Montgomery, Douglas C. et al. *Introduction to Linear Regression Analysis*. 3d ed. New York: Wiley, 2001.

Motulsky, Harvey. *Intuitive Biostatistics*. New York: Oxford, 1995.

Neyman, J. and Egon Pearson. "On the problem of the most efficient tests of statistical hypotheses." *Philosophical transactions of the Royal Society, Series A. 231* (1933) 289–337.

Oakes, Michael. *Statistical Inference*. Chichester: Wiley, 1986.

Oxman, Andrew, et al. "How to use an overview." No pages. Accessed July 6, 2007. Online: http://www.cche.net/usersguides/overview.asp.

Peto, Michael, et al. "Design and analysis of randomized clinical trials," *Br. J. Cancer 34* (1976) 585.

Popper, Karl. *The Logic of Scientific Discovery*. London: Rutledge, 1959.

———. "The problem of induction," 1974. In *A Pocket Popper*, edited by David Miller. London: Fontana Paperbacks, 1983.

Pratt, John. "Bayesian interpretation of standard inference statements" (with discussion), *Journal of the Royal Statistical Society, Ser. B* (1965) 169–203.

Rice, Martin. "What is a Science?" In *Contemporary Reflections on the Philosophy of Herman Dooyeweerd*, edited by DFM Strauss et al. New York: Edwin Mellen Press, 2000.

Royall, Richard. "The effect of sample size on the meaning of significance tests." *The American Statistician 40*: 4 (1986) 313–35.

———. *Statistical Evidence: A Likelihood Paradgm*. Boca Raton: Chapman & Hall, 1997.

———. "On the probability of misleading statistical evidence," *Journal of the American Statistical Association 95*: 451 (2000) 760–68.

Runner, H Evan. *The Relation of the Bible to Learning.* Jordan Station, Ontario: Paideia Press, 1982.

Ryan, Philip. *A Short Course in Elementary Biostatistics.* Adelaide, Australia: University of Adelaide, 2004. Accessed May 31, 2007. Online: www.health.adelaide.edu.au/publichealth/staff/ASCIEB_Chapter3.pdf.

Salsburg, David. "The religion of statistics as practiced in medical journals." *The American Statistician 39*: 3 (1985) 220–23.

Satherley, John. "Creation and the redemption of science." An address given at Portswood Church, Southampton, England, 1988.

Schaffner, Kenneth. "Ethically optimizing clinical trials." In *Bayesian Methods and Ethics in a Clinical Trial Design*, edited by Kadane. New York: Wiley, 1996.

Schield, Milo. "Using bayesian inference in classical hypothesis testing," *Proceedings of the 1996 Joint Statistical Meetings, Section on Statistical Education, American Statistical Association.* Accessed June 14, 2007. Online: http://www.augsburg.edu/ppages/~schield/MiloPapers/96ASA.pdf.

Schuurman, Egbert. "Beyond the empirical turn: responsible technology." No pages. Cited 2003. Online: http://home.wxs.nl/sch_art.htm.

Skillen, James. "Herman Dooyeweerd's contribution to the philosophy of the social sciences," *Journal of the American Scientific Affiliation 31* (1979) 20–24.

Stanford Encyclopedia of Philosophy. "Bayes' Theorem." No pages. Accessed June 20, 2007. Online: http://plato.stanford.edu/entries/bayes–theorem.

Sterne, Jonathan. "Teaching hypothesis tests–time for significant change?" *Statistics in Medicine 21* (2002) 985–94.

Sterne, Jonathan and George Smith. "Sifting the evidence–What's wrong with significance tests?" *British Medical Journal 322* (2001) 226–31.

Strauss, DFM. *Paradigms in mathematics, physics and biology: their philosophical roots.* Bloemfontein, South Africa: Tekskor Books, 2001.

Thompson, William. "402 citations questioning the indiscriminate use of null hypothesis significance tests in observational studies."

No pages. Accessed Nov 20, 2004. Online: http://biology.uark.edu/Coop/thompson5.html.

Torrance, Thomas. *The Ground and Grammar of Theology.* Harrisburg, Pennsylvania: Continuum Books, 2005.

US Federal Register, "Rules and regulations." Vol 67, No. 55, 13095–13098. Cited 2002. Online: http://www.fws.gov/policy/library/02fr13095.pdf.

US Fish and Wildlife Service. "Endangered and threatened wildlife and plants; determination of threatened status for the delta smelt." No pages. Accessed August 29, 2003. 50 CFR Part 17, 1993. Online:http://endangered.fws.gov/r/fr93492.html.

Ware, James. "P–values." In *Medical Uses of Statistics,* edited by John Bailar and Frederick Mosteller. Waltham, Massachusetts: NEJM Books, 1986.

Wright, Daniel. "Making friends with your data: Improving how statistics are conducted and reported." *British Journal of Educational Psychology 73* (2003) 123–36.

Yates, Frank. "The influence of 'Statistical Methods for Research Workers' on the development of statistics." *Journal of the American Statistical Association 46* (1951) 19–34.

www.ingramcontent.com/pod-product-compliance
Lightning Source LLC
Chambersburg PA
CBHW071622170426
43195CB00038B/2034